IT TAKES A VILLAGE

IT TAKES A VILLAGE

Navigating the Journey of

Parenting Your Autistic Child

Lhara Mullins

ORPEN PRESS

Published by
Orpen Press
Upper Floor, Unit B3
Hume Centre
Hume Avenue
Park West Industrial Estate
Dublin 12

email: info@orpenpress.com
www.orpenpress.com

Paperback ISBN 978-1-78605-171-4
ePub ISBN 978-1-78605-172-1

Printed in Dublin by SPRINTprint Ltd

This book is dedicated to my mother, Bernadette, aka 'Granny'. You mean the world to us.

FOREWORD

I feel happy about my Mam writing this book as it's an amazing opportunity for her and will allow people to learn more about people with autism. It will be helpful for parents of autistic children to have someone to relate to.

I feel like this book will help people with autism get an outside view of autism: to see how autism affects the people around them and the thought processes of their parents or caregivers. It will be especially helpful for parents of autistic children as it will give them an insight into other parents' lives and how to deal with certain situations.

Based on my experience of professionals working with families of autistic children, I think professionals need to listen to what the child needs and what the parents need and work on that. Sometimes I focused on things (therapies and approaches) which were not relevant to my needs when I was attending services. I felt some appointments didn't meet my needs. Another thing to note is that young parents or new parents might not know a lot about autism, but they're doing their best. When they come to any appointment this shows that they care and they want and need help for their child.

One thing I found very hard was sitting outside the room at appointments and knowing my parents and whoever we were there to meet were talking about me. Knowing that every little thing I did was talked about did, at times, make me wonder what was wrong with me. That was tough.

I would advise parents at the start of their autism journey with their children to really listen to what their child tells them they need. Most people with autism find it hard to communicate. So when your child tells you something, it's a big deal. Everyone with autism is different and all the signs and symptoms may not be the same for every child.

Ellie (Age 19)
February 2022

PREFACE

Three of our four children have autism: Ellie, who is nineteen; Alex, who is thirteen; and Daisy, who is eight. Our son Daniel is seventeen and neurotypical (NT).

I decided to write this book so that other parents of autistic children do not feel alone on their journey. I've navigated the murky system of getting a diagnosis of autism in Ireland three times now. And each experience was completely different, yet not one was straightforward.

The emotional toll of parenting an autistic child is something that's often swept under the carpet. Professionals often won't ask how you're coping, because they fear your honest answer. A large number of us feel like we're drowning, failing at parenting and that we can't do this anymore. We don't tell other parents or professionals about crying ourselves to sleep or that we've upped our dose of antidepressants to cope every day, in the midst of a broken system.

Then the guilt kicks in. Questions like: 'Why am I such a bad parent that I can't manage my child's behaviour?' 'How could I medicate my child at the age of seven?' 'Why do I jump when my phone rings when my child is somewhere without me?'

Welcome to this journey. First and foremost, I want you to know that if you are a parent of an autistic child, you *can* do this, you will get through it and your child will be okay. I say this to myself over and over as a mantra when things get tough. And things *do* get tough!

I decided a long time ago that I would eventually write this book. When I fumbled, scavenged and cried through my journey as a mother of an autistic child the first time around, I swore to myself that I would work towards using the hardest parts of my journey and what I've learned from it to help other families at the start of their own autism journey.

The system is broken. I wish I had known this earlier on and I wouldn't have kept hoping, or feeling optimistic even, that my children would get the care and intervention that they deserve. Fifteen years later, the system is different now that I am navigating it with my smaller children, yet it's still broken. I often think about what advice I would give to myself back then, or how I would do things differently. But I've come to realise that we, as parents, only have control over so much. With the exception of parents who can pay for private therapies for their autistic child (and even these are very hard to source), supports are few and far between, and only he/she who shouts the loudest gets heard.

In my personal life I think I'm seen as funny, outgoing and likeable. I think I'm seen similarly in my professional life. I'm bubbly and sociable in my job and I love my work. But as a mum of autistic children ... I am none of these things. I am *that* parent – the one who the professional needs to have downed two coffees before they see. I am *that* parent – the one whom whoever gets the short straw on the team has to meet with. I am the politely assertive mother who thinks she knows everything and will not stop calling, emailing and checking in, until my child's needs are assessed and a plan is in place to address them. I'm the 'tiger mom', the 'psycho mom' and definitely the mom every professional dreads making contact with. It took me a while, but now I'm perfectly okay with being all of these things. I am my child's voice. I am my child's hope. I am my child's advocate. I will never stop, no matter what. I am constantly trying to help my children to flourish and become whoever they want to be. But they need more help than my husband and I can give them. And the system in Ireland does not have the resources to meet all of their needs. But I will keep shouting the loudest, I will keep emailing and cc'ing multiple other professionals, and I will keep being the mom that everyone dreads to see, because that's exactly who my children need me to be.

So here you are, likely feeling worried, anxious, frightened and sad that you find yourself wondering if your child has autism. Or, you might be beyond relieved that you have finally identified what your child's needs are and how to help them. Or you may be reading this book because you feel hopeless, in a dark place and are wondering where the way out is.

I'm sharing my story of hope with you: my tales of the good, the bad and the absolutely heart-breaking... and sharing how after all of this I look at my four amazing and inspiring children and I feel beyond proud of each one. Their milestones may look different to what I had imagined, yet each of my children brings a unique, quirky and alternative zest into our family and into the world.

I am not speaking for my children, or taking the place of an autistic voice, as this voice deserves and needs to be heard in its own right. I am speaking here as a parent, with the aim of helping other parents to better cope as they try to meet their child's needs.

None of us are sailing through this, and that is the most important message to take from this book. We are all 'winging it' ... trying to get through each day and each week. So worrying about next year or five years from now won't serve you on this journey. Be the best you can be for today, to help your child to feel happy, included and loved.

ACKNOWLEDGEMENTS

This book was only a possibility on my horizon because of my beautiful babies. They teach me, lead me and open my eyes every day to their world and how they view it. I was able to write this book because of the journey my children have brought me on. I am amazed by their resilience, uniqueness and determination. And I am proud beyond belief of each of them for who they are and what they overcome daily to participate in a world not built for them and their needs. I'm grateful for the insight they give me into their neuro-divergently amazing perspectives. I'm grateful to Ellie especially for her blessing to write this book, and her understanding of my imperfections as a parent as she was our first child.

And thank you to Daniel. Thank you for taking a step back always, to let your siblings see. Thank you for your bear hugs towering over me and for loving Ellie so much, always. Your kind nature is such a beautiful characteristic. I love you.

To my (long-suffering) husband. Whatever my hair-brained scheme, wish or idea, you always, always support me. You say: 'Yes, you can do this'. You are my sounding board, you hold me up on the hardest of days and you trust my instinct consistently on how best to look after our children.

To my mother, Bernadette. Mam, we are beyond blessed to have you as a third parent to our children. You're my constant, my go-to person, my respite and my safety net. You care for my babies with as much love and protection as I do. Even though Daisy drives you insane! Thank you Mam for everything.

To my Dad, my Auntie Maureen and my four brothers. Thank you for being open to autism and all that our children have to teach you. Thanks for asking questions, and not batting an eyelid when this is exactly what we needed from you. Dad, thanks for loving each of our babies so very much.

To Auntie Carmel, thank you for keeping this secret! And for being proud of me always.

And to my people. I have the most wonderful real, honest and open friends. Each of you provide me with something unique, but each of you are consistent, long-term, long-time supportive friends.

To Nathalie, Fiona, Dana and Carol. I don't have sisters, but I am blessed to have the four of you.

A huge thank you to Eileen O'Brien and the team from Orpen Press. You made this process an enjoyable one and believed in my hopes for this book from day one.

To every single professional who has ever tried to help my children: thank you. To every teacher and SNA: thank you. Your role is so much more significant than maybe you know.

TABLE OF CONTENTS

INTRODUCTION

I was driving back from one of Ellie's appointments on my own with Ellie and Daniel strapped into their car seats in the back of the car. Ellie was three and Daniel was almost two. There's a road in Galway that's like a motorway, but very near the city centre so the speed limit is 50 km/hr. But nobody adheres to this. I was halfway up this road when I heard Ellie unclipping her car seat belt. I couldn't stop as there was no hard shoulder. I started coaxing her to get back in her seat. Within five seconds Daniel had crawled on to my lap while I was driving. Ellie had unclipped his car seat ... I had to stop. I checked my rear-view mirror and slowly stopped. I put on my hazards and started strapping both kids back in as fast as I could. I was sweating and panicking, aware that this was so dangerous. Finally, I jumped back into the front and check my rear view ... and then I heard it .... The sound of a truck horn and brakes screeching .... Everything froze. I could see the artic speeding towards us but I couldn't move so I braced for impact. The arctic screeched to a stop just inches from hitting my car. I sat there ... he sat there ... and I was shaking. The kids were oblivious. I waved out the window in apology, but the truck driver was as aware as I was that this was almost catastrophic. I drove home slowly. After going inside, I sat on the floor crying. I told my husband what happened. I didn't tell anyone else for years. I was embarrassed and I felt like I had almost killed my children – that I should, as a mother, be at least able to keep my children safe.

This was the worst day. Of all of my parenting experiences, this day haunts me the most. I still feel these feelings, and get that ball of fear in the pit of my stomach when I think about it.

This book will share a real, raw and honest experience of parenting autistic children. I will share the things no professional will advise you are even a possibility! And the things that even your best friend/Mom/Dad won't tell you. I will share our 'normal', so you can see that variations on this are completely okay. I'll share the proudest moments I've experienced with my kids, and how we as a family cope with the challenges that come with autism. I will share my 'how-to' tips based on my experiences. I'll share my mistakes and my reflections on challenges that we as a family are still struggling with. This book will also explore what the experts say on issues such as challenging behaviour, friends, socialising and what to do as a parent when you're not coping.

It's not always rainbows and butterflies, but this book will help you to find ways to meet your child's needs and cope with the rollercoaster that is being the parent of an autistic child. This book will help you to develop ways to protect, advocate for and enable the most important person in your world and find what makes them happy.

But please know that I don't have all the answers. I still struggle regularly with managing my own children, and by meltdown number five before 11 a.m. on a day of home-schooling, I am dreaming of wine myself! But I can hopefully help you to feel like you've found your tribe. Parents like us may feel as though we're struggling alone with our little people, but know that there's strength in numbers and we are in this together.

As a parent, autism is part of my family; it's a massive part of my life and will be forever. I feel this is a part of my identity as a mother and is something I consider first and foremost when planning anything or making any major decision. I can't emotionally or practically detach myself from autism, as this would mean detaching myself from my children and their needs. They can't always identify their own needs, or articulate these, so they need me to be their advocate when they need one.

What is the aim of this book?

This book aims to share with you some of the issues our family have struggled with the most during our journey with autism. It will identify feasible solutions and explore:

- The challenges you may face as a parent of an autistic child
- How you might tell your child about their autism diagnosis
- Ways you can help your child socially
- How an autism diagnosis is made in Ireland and the various steps involved in this process
- How you can best advocate for your child
- How to cope with challenging behaviour
- Coping with stress, depression and anxiety as a parent of an autistic child
- What we need from professionals we interact with
- How family and friends can help and not hinder you on this journey

How is this book presented?

Each chapter will start with some of my experiences relating to the topic being discussed. I will reflect on what worked, what definitely didn't work, and what I've learned from trying. Each chapter will then look at what the experts say regarding this topic and will finish with key points of learning. You can dip in and out, you can review a specific topic or browse the key learning points. Or you can strategically place this book where your friends and family members will see it if you want to subtly encourage them to see what you and your child are experiencing!

1

EARLY DAYS AND RED FLAGS

Introduction

This chapter will discuss some of the first signs of autism you may notice in your child. I will introduce you to each of our children who are on the spectrum and share their development from birth and the initial red flags we noticed. This chapter will discuss signs we can see now in hindsight, that we perhaps didn't see as relevant at the time. Not all the flags are red, however. They are often of varying colours! The signs of autism identified by experts will be explored and how you can support your child while awaiting assessment and diagnosis will also be discussed.

Our experiences

Ellie

Ellie was our first. Her birth was eventful, to say the least. I was nineteen years old and was three days overdue when my labour started. After a few hours, baby's heart rate was dropping. I was rushed for an emergency Caesarean section. Ellie was born silent. She needed some help to start breathing and a team of paediatricians were ready and waiting. After what seemed like a lifetime, we heard her cry. She was so beautiful. Ellie recovered quickly and came to the ward with me straightaway, and we left the hospital five days later.

All was normal for each of Ellie's developmental checks from this point. She was very bright, talked early on, and walked at fourteen months. Ellie didn't like sleep though. She woke up to ten times a night. We prayed every week and month that the sleeplessness was coming to an end ... but it wasn't. We used to lie in bed with her when she was a year old and pretend to sleep until she fell asleep. Sometimes this would take half an hour, other times this would take three hours. We used to then creep out of the room like a ballerina with the softest feet! And then her little head would pop up and we were back to square one. We took turns and tag-teamed on the harder nights. We didn't know any different. Ellie was our first, so we had no little person to compare her to. All her developmental checks to this point were normal, and verbally Ellie was surpassing expected milestones. She was super smart and would repeat words so clearly from about nine months old. We were beyond proud and enjoyed every moment with our little bright spark.

So this was normal life until baby number two, little Mr Daniel came along. Ellie was nineteen months old and a live wire by then. She was very smart, very articulate and seemed to be progressing on schedule developmentally. One particular day is so clear in my mind. Ellie was in her pushchair and came to the hospital to meet her new baby brother. I bent down and kissed her, talked to her and explained that her baby brother had arrived. I had had a Caesarean so I'm guessing in hindsight this is why we didn't take Ellie out of her pushchair initially. I asked her if she wanted to hold the baby and she said yes. I took Daniel from his crib and bent down to Ellie and placed him on her lap/chest. I held him close to her so she could see him. She muttered something I didn't quite hear. So I asked: 'What did you say, love?' Ellie replied, as clear as day: 'Get ... it ... off.' And this was the beginning of our journey in to the chaotic, mayhem, beautiful and enchanting journey of having an atypical child.

I felt immense guilt at this moment. I was 21 years old at this stage and I had two babies. I thought to myself 'Why did I do this to Ellie? Why did I not ensure she had time to just be, before having another baby?' I also thought that maybe this was normal. Ellie being a toddler and an only child and now having to share her world with this bizarre new little creature 24/7!

When Daniel and I came home from the hospital, we realised fairly quickly that Ellie was not happy with her little brother. She wouldn't cry, but would look with disgust at him and push him away. We found that we needed to supervise constantly to keep Daniel safe. Ellie was becoming increasingly mischievous. For example, she would throw toys and bottles at Daniel every day. We corrected her, gave her additional attention and tried 'time out' as we attempted to figure out what was normal and what wasn't. Then Ellie would hit baby Daniel or hit me and hit her Dad if we were holding Daniel. We were conscious that Ellie was only nineteen months old and was perhaps too young to understand what was expected of her behaviourally. Equally, our own young age as parents meant that we were learning as we went along.

However, as the months passed, the incidents of jealous behaviour towards Daniel increased in frequency and severity. One day I strapped Daniel into his car seat as I went to the bathroom. When I returned Ellie had turned the car seat upside down with Daniel still strapped in. Other times Ellie would try to cover Daniel's face with a blanket or towel and say: 'Baby gone!' We initially found these incidents hilarious and future content for wedding speeches and 21st birthdays. But as time went on, the incidents maintained momentum and we could see the danger Ellie was posing to Daniel. By the age of four months Daniel was sleeping through the night and was a very placid and easy-going baby. However, Daniel would visibly tense up when Ellie was near him. At 23 months Ellie was becoming increasingly challenging in her behaviour and was still waking five to ten times per night. We had enrolled her in a crèche for three hours per day twice a week before Daniel was born as we felt she needed more activities. The crèche staff found her use of language exceptional and were amazed by her vocabulary. Yet behavioural incidents started to happen in crèche and quite regularly. Ellie would hit, kick, scratch and eventually bite other children. She would gravitate towards one friend, but was unable to function as part of a group or triad of friends. Any variation of this would result in Ellie hurting other children or staff in the crèche.

Some more serious behavioural incidents occurred. When Ellie was young, she pushed Daniel down the stairs and knocked him unconscious. Ellie once tried to use a hand blender on Daniel's face (he still has a visible scar). She absconded from school, would run into traffic and there was generally chaos in our house through every minute of the day.

Initially, Ellie was suspected of having ADHD, and this was my thought too. The signs of autism were so slight upon first look and I would later learn that girls in particular, tend to mask the difficulties they have.

Alex

So baby number three came along. I was now 25 years old. Ellie was five and in school. And Daniel was four. Mr Alex was born via scheduled Caesarean section and was healthy at birth although he needed a little incubation for low temperature and blood sugars. His birth weight was average (6lb 6oz) and he was a lovely, calm-natured, beautiful baby boy. Off we went home after the usual five days in 2013 to start life as a family of five. Ellie seemed indifferent to Alex's arrival while Daniel was happy and interactive as we would have expected. When Alex was nine weeks old I spoke to one of our friend's at the school gate. He and his partner had had a baby a few weeks before we had Alex. I mentioned how Alex took breaks in his breathing when he was asleep and how this worried me, but we thought this was most likely normal. This Dad said that no, he didn't have this experience with his baby. I made a GP appointment the following day and explained my concerns. The GP checked Alex and he was above average weight for nine weeks old and appeared healthy. But we were sent to the hospital for a check as a precaution.

I was surprised when Alex was kept in for observation and the medical staff expressed concern for this breathing issue. Alex was fitted with an apnoea monitor and we were settled in for the night in the hospital room. The apnoea monitor would make an alarm sound if Alex's breathing stopped for ten seconds. I felt confident that it wouldn't stop for this length of time and I would be home with Alex the next day. I slept on a mattress on the floor. On the first night Alex's apnoea monitor sounded the alarm six times. Six times my tiny baby stopped breathing for ten seconds or more in one night. The next day Alex was sent for chest X-rays and was checked for mobility and cognitive red flags. All came back normal.

On night two, Alex's apnoea monitor alarmed four more times. No explanation was offered for this, but the terror it filled me with was indescribable. On night three, Alex's apnoea monitor was set to alarm at twenty seconds, as opposed to ten. The alarm did not sound. On day four in the paediatric ward, my husband and I were taught baby CPR and we were discharged.

Blood and urine samples had been taken from Alex and we were given an outpatient appointment for six weeks later. Two weeks later we got a call from the paediatric department. There was an anomaly/unexpected finding in Alex's urine test. We were asked to attend the next day to have the bloods and urine re-tested. Two weeks later we got another call. The urine test indicated a potential metabolic illness. We were given an appointment to attend Temple Street Children's Hospital in Dublin (a three-hour drive from where we lived) for metabolic testing. Alex's urine suggested a very rare and potentially dangerous metabolic condition, and they needed to test his urine when he was fasting and eating to gauge how his body coped with this. We spent two days in Temple Street and Alex was deemed to have some markers of a metabolic condition, but was largely asymptomatic. Alex was to be treated as an outpatient in Temple Street for the next few years and was identified as very much an anomaly for a child with a metabolic illness.

Alex was developing slowly. At nine months the GP diagnosed Alex as having global developmental delay. Alex was floppy, he had a head lag (his head just kind of flopped back when we picked him up), he couldn't weight bear on his legs and was not maintaining eye contact. Alex was referred for early intervention. Alex received occupational therapy and physiotherapy for the next year until at nineteen months, he eventually walked. We were super happy with Alex's progress and although he was delayed with motor skills and language development, overall he seemed well. Then at fifteen months Alex had his first episode of unconsciousness. Alex was sitting in his highchair when his eyes rolled back in his head and his head tilted back … and he was gone. He was unconscious. I screamed, scooped him up and shook him awake. He was drowsy but came around. I was hysterical. I went back to the hospital in Galway where we lived. All tests and examinations came back normal. Alex was given a test for epilepsy and this came back clear.

Coming closer to the age of two, Alex started having meltdowns. I remember calling Temple Street asking if this was a symptom of Alex's metabolic condition. The answer was that they didn't know. Alex started crèche and playschool and was quite average in his ability to interact and function. Alex was a gentle and kind-natured little person, he just needed extra help with tasks like getting dressed, brushing teeth and feeding himself. Alex slept well (despite the apnoea monitor) from about six months old.

Alex started school at age four. A mistake in hindsight. I should have waited and given him the additional year in preschool. Alex was blunt and said exactly what he thought. He had no insight into what was appropriate or what not to say. For example, Alex would tell people if he didn't like them, if he thought they smelled, or if they were overweight. The teacher noticed motor issues with handwriting, opening his pencil case and cutting with scissors. The teacher suggested Alex might have dyspraxia or Developmental Coordination Disorder (DCD) so he was referred for assessment. Within a few months Alex was diagnosed with DCD and we attended a disability service provider with him for occupational therapy classes to help him with buttons, zips and handwriting.

We slowly noticed Alex's behaviour changing as he got older. Tantrums turned into meltdowns with no end to them. And he became embarrassed easily and would shut down, completely disengage and scream non-stop. We still didn't for a moment suspect autism as Alex was so different to Ellie, they were not even remotely comparable. At a dentist appointment when Alex was ten, the dentist asked me if Alex had been assessed. And it was like a lightbulb moment. Everything just clicked into place. We had explained away awkward behaviours, meltdowns and bluntness as being part of DCD. But when I asked the dentist if she meant autism, she said yes and that she had a child herself on the spectrum. How on earth did I miss this?

Slowly issues began to emerge in school. Alex absconded from the class a few times, was very resistant to changes and was unable to take correction or see anyone else's perspective. Alex was in Fifth Class now. A psychologist and occupational therapist from his disability support services came to Alex's school to observe and concluded that a full autism assessment was needed. We were beyond blessed with Alex's disability services. They provided so many holistic and personal development supports which really helped Alex and us as a family.

Daisy

Third time around ... well by now, of course, we would know what autism looks like, right? You would think that. Daisy was a premmie, born at 35 weeks and had a low birth weight of 4lbs 7oz. Daisy spent her first few days in the Neonatal Intensive Care unit but came home on day six at 4lb 3oz. Daisy was a bit of a screamer from day one. I remember rushing up to feed her and waiting to be buzzed into the ward and I could hear this high-pitched scream. She sounded like a tiny feisty cat. When Daisy came home, Ellie, Daniel and Alex were all happy with her arrival. She didn't stir any major emotions for her siblings and we slowly adjusted to being a family of six.

Daisy had some reflux issues but gained weight quickly. One thing that didn't seem important at the time, but Daisy, just like Alex, had a head lag at her six-month developmental check. I didn't realise that this was significant until years later when I read about this. Apparently, this is an early indicator of a future autism diagnosis. Knowing at this point would have had little impact either way though. Like Alex, Miss Daisy was slow with her gross motor skills and was referred to the early intervention team by our GP. From the age of ten months until she walked at eighteen months, Daisy received occupational therapy and physio.

In hindsight, I brought Daisy to the GP frequently. She was often cranky and unsettled and never slept a night. Sometimes when I would see the GP, Daisy would have a throat or ear infection, but more often than not, there was no medical reason for her crankiness. Daisy woke every single night. It was exhausting. My husband and I would take turns as we both had work the next day, but really I was on duty. I chose this as I felt I could never truly trust anyone else in the world, even their Dad, to respond to their needs as well as I could. So I didn't sleep a night for three years. I remember sometimes driving to work after dropping the kids to crèche and school and not remembering bits of my journey. I was exhausted.

Sensory issues were probably the only consistent sign of autism in all of my children. But Daisy struggled the most. She could not bear how her underwear and socks felt and would have screaming tantrums daily when I tried to dress her. Daisy would tell people she didn't like them, ask them to leave when they were visiting our house and have screaming meltdowns because of how her clothes felt. Socks, underwear and trousers in particular caused Daisy such distress. Daisy was having regular meltdowns by the age of two and this continued after she started school aged four. However, in school, Daisy was absolutely angelic!

So I thought perhaps I was doing something wrong if this challenging behaviour was only happening at home. I would collect Daisy from school and she would pinch and scratch my hand before we even got to the car. Daisy would kick my seat the whole way home as she screamed. Yet in comparison to Ellie, Daisy's behaviour was mild. So I questioned myself and my parenting, rather than questioning a potential diagnosis. At age five however, as myself, my husband and Granny struggled to cope with Daisy's behaviour, I began to suspect ADHD.

The paediatrician at our very first visit when Daisy was six said she suspected autism. I was shocked and expressed this, as did my husband. But when the doctor explained what made her think this, slowly everything started to make sense. Daisy had very limited eye contact, was visibly uncomfortable with people speaking to her and most of her meltdowns were at times of transition (leaving the house, coming home from school, getting up in the morning, etc). These issues combined with the major sensory issues Daisy had with clothes, painted a picture of autism.

How did I not see this? We were in complete and utter shock!

Signs of autism in my children (in hindsight)

- Exceptional language development. Ellie spoke sentences from eighteen months and pronounced words with precision.
- Alex and Daisy both looked at the TV or at objects, from the side of their eyes. They would turn their head and look from the corner of their eyes.
- Stims: I didn't recognise these as stims at the time, but repetitive sounds, hand movements and head movements.

- Lack of interest in other children.
- Avoiding eye contact (or establishing eye contact only sometimes).
- Not looking at the camera in any family photos.
- Sensitivity to clothes, blankets, food and how they feel.
- Obsession with one particular toy or object.
- Lack of attempts to interact/happy to be alone.
- Waking at night past the age of six/eight months.
- Difficulty with changes (routine, new people, new furniture, new clothes).
- Noticing a dramatic difference in behaviour in an unfamiliar situation (a social event, school, an activity).
- Social awkwardness/inappropriateness.
- Direct speech/blunt communication.
- Head lag at six-month developmental check.
- Absolutely HATING haircuts! (This was an interesting one as I only realised how common this is after meeting other moms with kids on the spectrum).
- Birthdays or any major event causing intense distress.
- Fear of hand dryers in bathrooms.

Stims are self-stimulating behaviours some autistic children display. They are usually repetitive movements, sounds or actions. For Alex this was flapping his hands, rocking or pacing up and down (he still does this now and we don't discourage it). For Daisy this was repetitive hand movements, and for Ellie this was blinking incessantly, clearing her throat or grinding her teeth. Stims can cause concern when you see them at first. But stims help our children to make themselves feel more comfortable, if they are struggling with a sensory issue or social situation. Stims should never be corrected or discouraged. Anything that helps our little people to feel more comfortable (once it's not hurting anyone else), is okay.

How did I cope?

When I titled this book: *It Takes a Village*, I truly meant this. I have had the help of a third parent from the moment each of my children were born. This is the daily support and help I get from my own mother, Granny. I often wonder where I would be if I hadn't had this support especially when I often speak to other moms who have no support whatsoever. Since Ellie was born, Granny has provided respite once a week in the form of an overnight visit. I cannot stress enough how much this help has carried us through on the darkest days. I credit this regular respite with the fact that my marriage has survived the most turbulent times on this journey. I also know that my mental and emotional ability to parent my children has been massively enhanced by having this regular break.

I do feel judged by other parents, moms in particular, for having the luxury gift of respite. I find myself explaining my reasons for needing a break, or taking a holiday without my kids on a regular basis. But as I get older and I progress on this autism journey, I realise more that I don't need to explain myself, my parenting or my actions to anyone else. Having a full week off every year without the children has been what has got me through on the days I thought I couldn't go on. When I arrive at my GP's office and can't speak for the first ten minutes through my tears, I know I need this break. When I need sleeping tablets to get to sleep and anti-anxiety meds to get through a day, I know I need this break. Yet when I feel the judgement of another parent, the 'mom shame' starts immediately and I feel like a fraud or a failure.

This is still a work in progress for me. When I'm getting close to my break I can feel the cracks starting to show. My mood is low, my patience is short and I find myself crying at little incidents and unable to bounce back. But I am getting better at owning my family's story, our unique journey and what we do to get through. Each to their own. We need to do whatever we can to help our children on their journey. And as the saying goes, you cannot pour from an empty jug. So I try not to let other people's opinions, experiences or judgements in to my mental space. My children need me to be well, healthy and ready for anything. And regular respite from Granny helps me to do this.

Also, we all need a person. Each one of us needs one person we have as our go-to. This can be a family member, a friend or a professional. Having a person helps you to feel like someone truly hears you. We can talk to different people about our day-to-day struggles, but we just need one person who we feel truly understands. Find your person.

What the experts say

There is a wealth of information available for you to read up on autism and get a better understanding of what this will mean for your child and your family. This section will provide a brief overview of what autism means from some of the evidence gathered to date. Autism is known as a developmental disorder which affects communication and behaviour.[1] Autism is present in children before the age of three, can impact on their ability to socialise and can cause repetitive behaviours.[2] High-functioning autism affects one in every 270 children.[3] The term 'Asperger's' was first identified in 1944 by Hans Asperger and was used to describe children who had social difficulties, but were quite high functioning.[4] 'Asperger's' or 'high-functioning autism' describes children of normal intellectual ability and is sometimes referred to as a mild form of autism.[5]

The terms 'neurodivergent' and 'neurotypical' are now widely used when referring to people's differences concerning how our brains work. 'Neurodivergent' or 'neurodiverse' are words used to describe an individual or group whose brain works differently from what is considered typical, while 'neurotypical' refers to an individual whose brain is considered typical neurologically.

Since 2013, the term 'Autistic Spectrum Disorder' (or ASD) replaced all previous variations such as 'high-functioning autism' and 'Asperger's'.[6] ASD uses a scale to identify the severity of the disorder.[3] Children with high-functioning autism will likely be diagnosed with ASD level one, which means they require support in their daily lives. Children with level two ASD require substantial support. And children with level three ASD require very substantial support.[7] Many parents, professionals and autistic individuals do not find the scale or measurement of severity helpful. I actually do, but this is a personal preference based only on my own experiences.

Autistic children struggle with processing sensory stimuli, which means that sounds, sights, smells, touch and taste can cause them distress.[6] ASD can mean that children can become obsessed with certain objects, ideas or activities to the degree that this affects their ability to function.[5] For example, some children may become over-fixated with dinosaurs and this could be the only topic they will discuss, or will only play with dinosaur toys, read dinosaur books or draw or paint dinosaurs when they are colouring.

Co-morbidities are quite high with autism. This means that the likelihood that an autistic child will also have another disorder such as depression, anxiety or ADHD, is high.[8] Although, in medical terms autism is identified as a syndrome and a disorder.[2] Autism can be to you and your child whatever you choose it to be. All children have vulnerabilities and things that they find more challenging, so autism shouldn't define your child or what they can accomplish.[9] However, getting a diagnosis of autism can help you to support your child to reach their full potential, and feel less distress in situations which challenge them.[9] The more we know about our children and their needs, the better we can help and support them to be who they want to be.

Having a good understanding of the signs of autism can help you to have your child assessed and diagnosed at an earlier age.[10] It is important to note that autism is four times more common in boys than in girls.[10] Frequent temper tantrums, aggression and the need for things to stay the same are some key signs which may indicate the possibility of autism.[11] Having your child's autism diagnosed as early as possible can positively impact your child's outcomes. The earlier interventions are put in place to support your child, the better for them in the long run.[12] Equally, when a diagnosis is made, this may help to relieve some of the stress you may be feeling as a parent,[12] and consequently enable you to be the best parent you can be.

Some studies have found that signs of autism in young children who are diagnosed later in life, can be evident looking back at family videos.[13] Noticeable clues might be a child not responding to their name, avoiding eye contact and not looking at a camera for a photo or video.[13] Other early signs might be a child who becomes distressed due to sounds, smells or how things feel, or if a child is overly obsessed with certain things or objects.[14] Some autistic children may have a flat tone to their voice and may not have a desire to interact with you or with other children.[14] Autism is sometimes missed in young children and a diagnosis may not be made until the child starts school, or even in adulthood. This can be because they may not show the signs and symptoms normally associated with autism, until they experience certain stressors such as social situations. Finally, it's important to know that autistic children can and do develop and progress with intervention and support.[3] Equally, many autistic children do make eye contact and masking (discussed in a later chapter) can also mean that some children may not display the more obvious characteristics usually identified with an autism diagnosis.

What can you do to help your child and your family while you are on a waiting list for assessment or services?

From the very start of my journey with all three of my autistic children (pre-diagnosis), I attended my GP on a regular basis. This was a lifeline for me. It was a professional I could express my concerns to and someone who could document these concerns to share with other professionals who could help my children. Ask for the same GP each time where possible – having this person who knows you and your child is so helpful. And if you are feeling depressed, low, anxious or hopeless, do share this with your GP and know that you won't be judged.

Ask family members or close friends for help. The hardest part of parenting is admitting to ourselves or other people that maybe we're not coping. This is perfectly okay and will actually really help your child in the long run. Ask a family member to have your child for a sleepover, to babysit, to let you have a shower or go out for a walk on your own, or just to spend time with you and your children and share some of the responsibility (particularly if you are parenting alone).

You can self-refer for family support: this is available in your local resource or community centre. Just phone, email or pop in to them in person, and they will see what resources they have which could help your family. Examples of what family support may offer include: homework and afterschool clubs for your child, one-to-one support for you as a parent, parenting courses and even practical advice around budgeting and diet.

If you are really struggling to manage your child's needs and feel like you need extra help and don't have this available, you can refer yourself to TUSLA, the child and family agency. Many parents have a fear of TUSLA and social workers in general. But contrary to popular belief, social workers are there to help children and parents, and *very rarely* remove children from their homes. For example, if you have no family support and would really benefit from respite, TUSLA can help to match you with a family who can offer respite. They may share their home with your child at the weekend, or for a longer time if needed. Social workers can also help parents to cope with their own mental-health issues and link families in with support services where they can access help.

Self-care is key! Find what works for you and make yourself do this. This could be yoga on YouTube, meditation, having a long bath alone, going for a walk or meeting a friend for coffee. The harder things become with managing your child's needs, the less you will feel like doing any of these self-care tasks. But this is when you need to look after yourself the most! We have little control over our children's needs, their behaviours or the challenges that come on this journey. We can control how we react though, and this is a powerful realisation.

Try counselling. This may sound like a bizarre suggestion, but I firmly believe everyone should have a counsellor. It's a place you can go to and completely offload your feelings. It's a person outside of your family and friends who will really listen and help you to process your own feelings and emotions. Counselling can be in person or online, and affordable counselling is now much more readily available. Counselling has got me through some of the darkest days and has given me the resources to cope when I felt like I couldn't.

Take the easy option some days. If your child is distressed because of their clothing, let them wear their pyjamas. If you are attending an event and your child is hysterical in the build up to this, sit this one out or get a babysitter. If you're having a day where you feel you can't get out of bed just do the best you can do for that day and make plans for a better day tomorrow. Give yourself a break. Be kind to yourself. The best gift you can give your child is being a happy and healthy parent. The small things won't matter in the grand scheme of things.

Find groups for parents of autistic children so you can connect with other people who know exactly how you feel. There are lots of online groups available and sometimes just hearing other people's experiences can help you to feel less alone. Online groups are a great place to get tips and advice, and an opportunity for you to socialise and meet new people.

KEY LEARNING POINTS FROM THIS CHAPTER:

- No two autistic children will present with the same needs. This makes autism difficult for parents to recognise, even if they already have a child with a diagnosis of autism.
- The signs and symptoms of autism are many. Communication difficulties and distress with changes are common signs of autism in children.
- High-functioning autism used to be called Asperger's Syndrome. Now ASD level one is the diagnosis given to autistic children who present with typical intellectual ability.
- Stims may be your child's way of trying to feel more comfortable when they feel stressed.
- Take respite whenever you can and seek this out of you don't have family support. Looking after yourself is key to enabling you to look after your child.
- If you are late recognising the signs of ASD, that's okay and don't dwell on this. Focus on what's next on your journey of helping your child to progress.
- Join groups online to connect with other parents who understand what you're going through. Some of the most insightful advice I've ever received, has been from moms I've met on Facebook.

Conclusion

This chapter has provided a snapshot and initial insight into autism and what this means for our family. Long before I knew any of my children were autistic, I met their needs based on their individual personalities, likes and dislikes. And you are most likely doing the same. Every autistic child presents completely differently. And even the most expert person in the world could miss the signs of autism in their own child. Because to us they're just them, they're our babies. They are unique, beautiful and so loved. In hindsight, I can see now a lot of signs that I didn't realise were signs. Sensory issues, in particular with clothing, stand out. Fussy eating habits and sleep problems were further warning signs, as were challenges with coping when a change or unexpected event happened. Some autistic children miss developmental milestones, while others meet or exceed these. If you suspect your child might be autistic, mention this to your GP and they can help to identify if assessment is needed. And rest assured, an autism assessment (between waiting and the assessment) can take up to three years. So nothing will change overnight and you and your child will have plenty of time to process their needs and an eventual diagnosis. But more than anything, know that you know your child and what they need, and you are enough.

2

THE WINDING ROAD TO DIAGNOSIS

Introduction

This chapter has been by far the most difficult to write. Because there simply is no clear pathway to assessment and diagnosis of autism in Ireland. This chapter will discuss the avenues each of my children experienced in their autism assessment and diagnosis journey. I will identify the possible methods you can employ when you suspect your child is autistic and how you can best try to access an assessment. The pros and cons of a public versus a private assessment for your child will be discussed. This chapter will also examine the research around autism diagnoses and the process which is undertaken prior to a diagnosis of autism being made.

My experiences

Ellie

Ellie had the most complex pathway to eventual diagnosis of autism out of my three children. I suspect this is partly because this was back in 2006 when we were first referred and knowledge and understanding about autism and its prevalence wasn't as advanced as it is now. Equally, Ellie's masking ability likely also contributed. Having ADHD further made autism more difficult to see externally.

I had been expressing concerns about Ellie's behaviour to my GP since a few weeks after Daniel was born. Initially I was just discussing concerns, but as time went on and the challenging behaviour increased, my GP made a referral to children's mental health services for investigation of potential ADHD. This was what I suspected would be the diagnosis and autism at this point wasn't even on my radar. After waiting for a few months, Ellie was seen and we attended regular assessment sessions with two doctors. We talked about incidents of serious behaviour and how we could respond to this and help Ellie. Being young and naïve, I didn't for a moment realise that this was not an assessment and was more of a family support appointment. I was in fact seeing a social worker and social care worker and exploring ways of increasing my coping capacity. One day when I was particularly upset discussing another incident of Ellie opening Daniel's car seat buckle while I was driving, the professional suggested I give her a bag of sweets while I'm driving. This was when I realised 'Okay... something is amiss here!' This absolutely could have been explained to me at the start of these sessions, but if it was, I have no memory of this. My own preconceived ideas of what to expect meant I had no real idea what we were actually there for or the goal of the appointments. I most likely wrongly assumed that it was a child psychiatrist I was seeing. Eventually we did meet with a doctor and Ellie was diagnosed initially with ODD or oppositional defiant disorder. ODD is described by the American Psychiatric Association[15] as a behavioural condition where the child intentionally defies adults or authority figures, is disobedient and generally behaves in a negative way which is not appropriate for their age.

It would be three years before Ellie was eventually diagnosed with ADHD. But in this time the service we were attending conducted assessments of Ellie in school, in person and with us as parents. They were quite proactive in working with us to find a diagnosis and help Ellie to manage better in school and at home. Ellie received occupational therapy and play therapy and her sensory issues were highlighted. Ellie really struggled with the textures and feel of clothing, socks, and shoes in particular could result in considerable distress (screaming and flailing). It was noted that there were some indicators of autism, but at this time, not enough for a diagnosis. We continued receiving services aimed at ADHD and social issues from the children's mental health provider. Ellie attended social skills groups, had a detailed assessment in a school for children with mental health issues and her team worked closely with her school teachers and SNAs to help Ellie. In hindsight, we were quite fortunate with the therapies and services we received at this time and we really felt like we had a 'go-to' person at all times on Ellie's team, whom we could contact if we needed to.

We still had daily challenges with behavioural issues and Ellie regularly hit and hurt other children. It was really tough on her. She was trying so hard but just struggled to conform or understand what was expected of her socially. When she was eleven years old, we went to Dublin to see a child psychiatry professor (who has since retired) and obtained a private diagnosis of autism for Ellie. We also got a public diagnosis about two years later via Ellie's existing service provider. So as you can see, the process for Ellie and for us was gruelling at times. But I did feel supported by professionals. I didn't think they got things right every time, but they were there with us and kept trying to help. Also, I could pick up the phone if I needed to and someone would always call me back. This was a lifesaver at times. Even the receptionist in Ellie's service provider became a familiar source of support! Often, we don't recognise the value and significance of a kind voice on the phone – this is someone who is at the forefront of children's services.

Figure 2.1: Pros and cons of private diagnosis

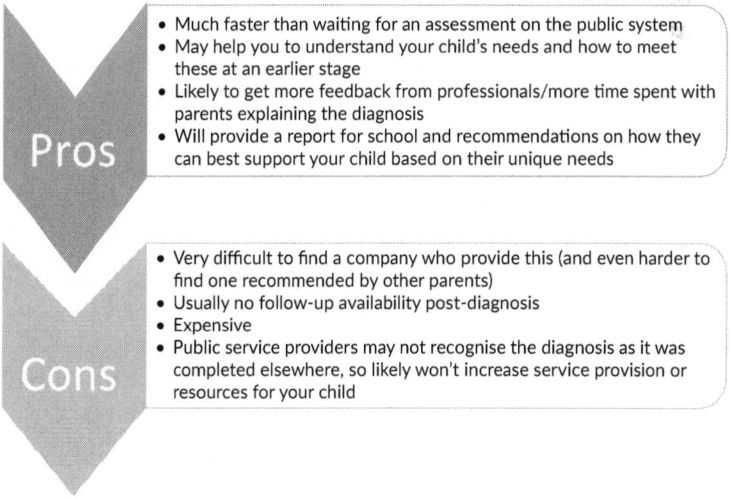

Pros
- Much faster than waiting for an assessment on the public system
- May help you to understand your child's needs and how to meet these at an earlier stage
- Likely to get more feedback from professionals/more time spent with parents explaining the diagnosis
- Will provide a report for school and recommendations on how they can best support your child based on their unique needs

Cons
- Very difficult to find a company who provide this (and even harder to find one recommended by other parents)
- Usually no follow-up availability post-diagnosis
- Expensive
- Public service providers may not recognise the diagnosis as it was completed elsewhere, so likely won't increase service provision or resources for your child

Many parents wonder if it's a good idea to go down the route of seeking a private diagnosis. I've outlined the pros and cons of this based on my experiences in the model on page 19.

Alex

Alex's road to diagnosis was a very winding one. Alex had got a diagnosis of Developmental Co-ordination Disorder (DCD), also known as dyspraxia when he was five. So he has difficulty with gross motor skills like dressing himself, handwriting and organisational skills. Alex had been in receipt of early intervention services prior to this for global developmental delay. Alex was quite floppy as a baby, he had little muscle tone and was behind with his developmental milestones. But as soon as he caught up and started walking at nineteen months old, he was discharged from their services.

Alex's teacher noticed some fine motor skills deficits when he was in Junior Infants. Alex would struggle with holding a pencil, writing, using scissors, etc. So once he was diagnosed with DCD we received disability support services. We, along with Alex, attended different classes for specific motor skills such as tying shoes, doing buttons, etc. He did act up at these classes though, which was quite out of character as he got older. Alex would sit under the table or refuse to participate. We were surprised and Alex was so easy-going normally. However, Alex always needed extra help. He was and still is the gentlest soul. But Alex needed guidance consistently to complete tasks and would still need assistance with things like dressing himself. He didn't like change and in particular I remember when we changed our car, he couldn't get his head around this. He would ask why did we do this? The other car wasn't broken, he liked the other car and could we get it back?

But still, Alex's needs were so different to Ellie's, so I genuinely didn't consider for a second that he might be autistic. But the day at the dentist when I finally realised that Alex was probably more typically autistic than Ellie ever was, we started pushing for an assessment immediately. I self-referred for an Assessment of Need (AON) through the HSE. An assessment of need is for any child with a disability or suspected disability and is a comprehensive assessment of their needs.[16] The AON then provides a report with your child's needs identified and recommendations for services or further assessments. The AON does not (according to the HSE website) provide diagnoses, and instead identifies if a child might need an assessment and within which service.[16] Our GP, after meeting with Alex and listening to my concerns, also referred Alex for an AON.

The HSE contacted our existing disability service provider, who within a few months had done a school observation visit with Alex, spoken to me at length and spoken to Alex's teacher. This was a team of two professionals: an OT and a child psychologist. Both agreed that Alex did indeed require an official autism diagnosis and we were put on the waiting list for the ASD team in Galway for an assessment. Then nothing happened for two years. The pandemic hit after almost a year of waiting and then the ASD team was discontinued. Daisy (even though she was waiting less than a year) was assessed and diagnosed while Alex was still waiting. I could have got a private diagnosis for Alex at this point. But the reason I didn't is because all of his needs were being met. Alex was still under the disability support team due to his DCD, so we had a provider we could ask for advice/support. In primary school, and more recently since the transition to secondary school, Alex's teachers and school staff have been providing his education and care based on his needs as an individual, regardless of diagnosis. We have been beyond lucky with all of our children to have the most supportive and exceptional school support. So eventually, towards the end of the pandemic lockdown, Alex was assessed for autism (via an outsourced private provider sourced via the HSE AON). The assessment was all completed online via video link. So it was no surprise after this time when Alex received his official autism diagnosis at the age of thirteen. Thankfully, nothing needed to change. At home and at school Alex was getting the right supports and encouragement to meet his needs. I do think the remote assessment was a really efficient (and yet still very thorough and professional) way of reducing waiting lists for children for autism assessments. The current system is not working, so we need to change it!

I often think about and have spoken to other parents who don't have the support network I have and who continue to struggle alone with their child while they await assessment. Children may be struggling with communication, incontinent, waking frequently at night, or maybe self-harming (biting or head-banging), or hurting other people in their families. I imagine that each day waiting for assessment and intervention for these families, feels like a week.

Daisy

With Daisy, we had been seen at our public health nurse's clinic by the paediatrician when she was three. The paediatrician did at this point prescribe Melatonin. It was such a relief having only slept one full night in over three years. The paediatrician we saw didn't have any major concerns for Daisy and we agreed we would take a wait-and-see approach. Daisy was having absolutely no obvious issues in crèche or pre-school and when she eventually started school. However, now I can see that she was masking. We would have 30-minute meltdowns which would start before we even got in the car after school.

I visited my GP again when Daisy was six and we agreed that it was time to make a referral. My GP referred Daisy for a psychology assessment and then we went back to the paediatrician we visited when Daisy was a baby (being a preemie and being behind with her milestones). I also, applied for an Assessment of Need (AON) through the HSE.

Daisy is nine at the time of writing. We are still waiting for that psychology appointment. But thankfully, due to having a very intuitive and autism-aware paediatrician, combined with having applied for the AON, meant that thanks to the efforts of the paediatrician and an AON psychologist (specifically for AON assessments), Daisy was diagnosed last year with autism at age seven. This was by far my most straightforward and least stressful road to diagnosis with any of my children.

The care and support was so well organised and cohesive that the paediatrician and psychologists – who work for completely different teams – came together to meet with Daisy, my husband and I, to discuss her diagnosis. It was one of those Oprah 'A-ha!' moments for sure. There was an OT also at this meeting who we weren't expecting. We expected to meet two people and there were three. Daisy went into shutdown. She wouldn't speak, wouldn't look at any of them and covered her face with her coat for the first half an hour. It was so typical of autism. All of us in that room knew that there was absolutely no doubt in the world that Daisy was autistic. They sat with us for two hours and went through everything from the assessment, to what's next and also explained Daisy's diagnosis to her and were available to answer any questions. It was such a profound experience, so positive, so proactive and so empathetic. We left feeling well cared for and that Daisy really mattered to them.

What is masking?

Masking, also known as social camouflaging, is when your child works extremely hard to make their autistic traits less obvious, and fit in with other children.[17] Masking behaviours might include outwardly coping or engaging when finding things extremely diffi-cult, or could be mimicking the behaviour of other children to fit in. Hull and colleagues report that masking is more common in females, and can contribute to a later or even a missed diagnosis. Masking can also increase mental health difficulties for autistic people and is very difficult and challenging to engage in long-term.[18] Some of the reasons autistic people camouflage have been identified as: trying to appear as what you think is expected of you, trying to be accepted by other people and attempts at 'fitting in and passing as neurotypical'.[18] When you think of this in the context of a small child, it's actually heart-breaking. Imagine feeling such pressure to change how you are and who you are, to feel accepted by other children?

Ellie and Daisy both mask extremely well. So much so that sometimes when they come home from school, or a friend or family member leaves our house, I can visibly see the mask slip. They revert back to who they are naturally and don't need to pretend or mimic. The effort this takes is immense.

Pearson and Rose[19] suggest that masking occurs when the indi-vidual is responding to the expectations of them imposed by society and negative views about autism generally. More well-known and perhaps stereotyped symptoms of autism such as not making eye contact, or being exceptional on a specific topic, may be the things an autistic child actively hides. Pearson and Rose[19] propose that this is not choice based or something the person necessarily wants to do, but the child more so does this to avoid potential rejection or exclusion.

How is autism assessed and diagnosed? What the experts say

An autism diagnosis is a process, and usually take multiple visits and meetings with different professionals. Different methods of assessment are undertaken such as parent interviews, child interviews, reports from teachers and observation of your child in person. Waiting lists for assessment, in addition to the time it takes to commence and complete the assessment, can take a considerable amount of time.

An autism assessment is usually undertaken by two or more professionals and should include gathering detailed assessment on your child's development, investigation of your child's communication, behaviour and interests.[20] [21]

The Diagnostic and Statistical Manual of Mental Disorders (commonly known as the DSM) is the most fundamental or core measurement tool for autism assessment and diagnosis.[22] Detailed assessment relating to very specific criteria are scored based on the DSM and this score dictates whether or not your child is diagnosed with autism.[23]

Areas of your child's life which are assessed include:

- Verbal and non-verbal communication
- Restrictive and repetitive behaviours/interests
- Sensory processing
- The need for sameness
- Social interaction

Only when these specific criteria produce scores indicative of autism will an autism diagnosis be made.[23] The CDC[24] clarify that the DSM must indicate persistent deficits which are considered severe in order for a diagnosis of autism to be made. For example, the communication difficulties must have been observed/

experienced for a substantial time frame, and such difficulties must be severe enough to impair your child's ability to interact and cope with their everyday life.

Such specific and substantial criteria for an autism diagnosis serve to ensure that diagnoses are indeed accurate and that errors in diagnosis are very unlikely. I think most people (myself included before my own family's experiences) perhaps don't realise the extent to which difficulties must be present prior to an autism diagnosis being made. It's not 'easy' to meet the criteria for an autism diagnosis. Equally notable is the continued development of the DSM. The DSM currently being used to assess children is the 5th edition. The manual is reviewed and revised continually to reflect and incorporate developments in research and understanding concerning mental health and illness.[24]

However, there are criticisms regarding the use of the DSM. Lynch[25] reports that the interpretation of the professional administering the assessment can create variation in how the DSM is used or applied. While criticisms of the DSM go as far as to suggest that using this manual could result in as much as 50% of the population being diagnosed with a mental disorder.[26] Yet I think that most people, unless they experienced significant difficulties with interaction, would take the time to refer and wait for an autism assessment.

Other assessment tools which may be used by the professionals undertaking your child's autism assessment may also include:

Autism Diagnosis Observation Schedule (ADOS): an assessment tool which is based on observation of your child in person, via activities and prompts introduced by the examiner.[27] The ADOS takes 30 to 60 minutes to complete and enables the examiner to see first-hand your child's ability to communicate and problem solve.[27]

Autistic Diagnostic Interview Revised (ADI-R): a detailed interview with parents to assess your child's needs and abilities. The ADI-R is a very detailed and specific interview and is administered by a trained professional.[28] The professional then scores your answers and this helps to identify the likelihood of a potential autism diagnosis.[28]

A large UK study in 2016 with over 1,000 parents participating found that parents usually waited at least a year after initially suspecting their child may have autism prior to speaking to a professional.[29] Crane and colleagues further report that the average time between approaching a professional and a diagnosis of autism was three-and-a-half years.[29]

The majority of parents report feeling a sense of relief after their child is diagnosed with autism according to Mansell and Morris.[30] This relief is relating to understanding the reason for challenging behaviours and with feeling they could access the supports their child needs.[30] Ozonoff and colleagues[31] suggest that parents of a child already diagnosed with autism, are often better at identifying early signs of ASD in their subsequent children (not the case for me!). But they also argue that in retrospective studies when parents look back signs of autism are often evident from about the age of one.[31] Equally, professional knowledge and understanding of ASD is really important in early identification in children, and subsequently, more timely assessment.[32] While some professionals may be hesitant in identifying signs of ASD in children if they are not competent in their knowledge of autism and feel they are not sufficiently trained.[32]

One study published in 2021 and based on autism diagnosis in the UK, describes the process as a very unique and narrative journey which often isn't clear cut.[33] Hayes and colleagues report that diagnosis of autism cannot be done through any specific testing method and instead is based on multiple detailed assessment tools and observations, and then piecing these together to create a picture of the child.[33]

So how exactly do you get an autism assessment for your child?

I really wish I could answer this question clearly and concisely. But the truth is, in Ireland at present, this is not clear cut. As you have read above, my three children had three completely different routes to eventual diagnosis. Daisy's was the most straightforward. But equally, I suspect we were just very lucky with the paediatrician we met and how knowledgeable she was about autism.

First and foremost when you first notice red flags or feel concerns in the back of your mind, speak to your GP or public health nurse.

No immediate action or referral is taken at this point, but they will be able to note your concerns, discuss these with you and monitor your child's development as necessary from this point. If your GP or nurse feels there are red flags, they will make a referral to the service they think is most appropriate. For example, when children are attending public health nurse developmental screenings up to the age of three, paediatricians can review children in this clinic if autism is suspected.

You can also be referred to the paediatrician at your local hospital or to a psychologist in the community for an assessment of your child's needs. You could be referred for early intervention if your child hasn't started school yet. Or you might be referred for a specific therapy such as speech and language therapy if your child has difficulties communicating, or to physiotherapy if your child's motor skills are presenting concern. None of these referrals will result in an immediate autism assessment though. The process is very slow and very detailed and looks at all other possible causes for your child's needs too.

Where you live in Ireland or the UK will further impact the route of assessment and diagnosis for your child. Alex waited two years for assessment, while Daisy waited just one year. The availability of clinicians in more rural areas is problematic. In Ireland, existing service providers for children with disabilities have been amalgamated as of 2021 and are now known as the Progressive Disability Service (PDS). The restructuring of the disability support services to become one core service will hopefully and eventually make this journey much more straightforward and mainstream. The PDS programme is a streamlined disability service provider which aims to meet all of the child's needs from a team perspective, rather than children receiving services from multiple different providers.[34] For example, previously children might have attended one service for physiotherapy and a different service for psychology. Whereas now the child will have one team of professionals co-ordinating their care and communicating with one another. I am hopeful that PDS will improve service provision and result in a more cohesive service all under one roof. I have to be hopeful.

KEY LEARNING POINTS FROM THIS CHAPTER:

- Waiting lists for ASD assessments are one to two years (based on my experiences) and waiting lists for therapies are even longer.
- Private assessment for autism is possible and results in a faster diagnosis, but can be expensive.
- Autism is assessed based on specific investigative tools such as the DSM and ADOS.
- Specific areas for assessment of autism relate to: communication, the need for sameness and repetitive behaviours.
- An autism assessment is usually based on the expertise and observation of at least two different professionals.
- Substantial and prolonged difficulties have to be present for an autism diagnosis to be made.
- Your GP and public health nurse are the first point of contact when you have concerns about your child or suspect they may be autistic.

Conclusion

This chapter discussed the very different roads to an autism diagnosis experienced by my family. The process can be exhausting in itself and this can take its toll on parents as well as children. Private autism assessment can result in a faster diagnosis than waiting on the public list. Yet there are both advantages and disadvantages to going down the private route. Also discussed in this chapter were the multiple steps parents can take when they suspect their child may have ASD. Masking is a common reason for a delay in diagnosis of ASD. While specific criteria based on the DMS and the clinical evaluation of two or more professionals is usually how autism is assessed and diagnosed in children. The first port of call for information and referral is your GP or public health nurse. More than anything, do share your concerns sooner rather than later with your healthcare provider. The earlier issues are raised, the earlier supports can be put in place.

3

PROCESSING YOUR OWN FEARS AND WORRIES

Introduction

This chapter will discuss the fears that many parents feel when they first suspect their child may be autistic, when they are going through the diagnosis, and after the diagnosis. There's no one right way you should expect to feel. You may find yourself coping with your emotions and the emotions of other family members while still responding to your child's needs. You may find yourself struggling to come to terms with a diagnosis or potential diagnosis while still responding to your child being in distress or ongoing challenging behaviour. Autism doesn't just affect one member of a family. It affects the whole family. It changes your life and the life of your child. And you both slowly adjust to what this means for them and how you can best help and support them. But it is hard! It is emotionally challenging, it's heart-wrenching at times and can be absolutely exhausting because of how much you love your children.

With my first child, I felt such absolute sadness that she may struggle throughout her childhood and into her adult life. Why did she have to suffer in school every day sitting alone? Would this ever get better? Would she have friends? I wanted to wrap her up and hold her forever to protect her from the world that just seemed so cruel to her and so confusing.

For my second, I felt so shocked at the suggestion he may be autistic, and immense guilt that I hadn't suspected this. I wondered if I was a terrible parent? I mean how on earth did I not see this? While for little Miss Daisy I was the most shocked. I didn't see this coming in a million years as she is so good at masking. Then I felt a whole new wave of emotions, realising I now had three autistic children and a neurotypical child. So there really is no right or wrong way to feel.

My experiences

I felt immense guilt. I wondered if it was something I had done or hadn't done. Was it in my family history? Was it due to my parenting? As we don't know the cause of autism and we deal with the long road to diagnosis, we can often just feel like we're not parenting in the right way or that we're failing.

I've felt loss. I've grieved not for myself, but for my children and some of the things they may struggle with and may never be able to achieve in their lives. But this has developed over the years into sheer determination. Now nothing is off the cards and they can do absolutely anything they want in their lives and I will support them. Nonetheless, loss is a normal emotion to feel when you think your child might not be the person you expected them to be, or the person they hope to be themselves. Some autistic children may not live independently without supports, or may not drive a car or travel on their own as adults. Grieving for these losses or potential losses I think is our body's way of preparing ourselves for our future with our children and what this might be like. Processing these feelings is a way of reducing the upset we may feel as milestones happen or don't happen later in life for our children.

I've felt shock. You do get a shock when you get a diagnosis of autism, or if a healthcare professional or a family member mentions the word, especially if you hadn't considered this as a possibility. It can happen! As Alex had dyspraxia, I put a lot of his difficulties down to that. It was actually one of the loveliest dentists who made the suggestion in a very kind and subtle way by just asking if he had been assessed. It was such a shock at the time. I was so disappointed with myself because, in hindsight, it was obvious. But we don't always notice with our own children. I see it in in other children and often even in adults. I notice autistic traits. But I missed it with two of my own children. Some parents have no inkling anything might be different about their child and the shock can cause such upset and distress for them. And shock can still happen when an official diagnosis is made even after a lengthy and detailed assessment. Hearing those words and seeing a diagnosis on paper is very different to just suspecting it. Even if it confirms what you knew deep down, it can still knock you.

The fear of the future has been a massive thing to process and it is ongoing. I used to lie awake at night in bed and wonder: 'What would happen to my children if I died today? Who would care for them the way I do? Who would love them as much as I do and really know their needs? Who would encourage them, know when to step in or step back and let them do something for themselves even when they're struggling?' And then the worry about adulthood. This is a tough one. 'Will they live independently? When my husband and I die, who will help them as adults?' My mam will be gone by then too. There's one of my children in particular who will need fairly substantial support across their life and most likely will not live independently. I have visions of them living alone, not able to take care of themselves. Horrible visions. The worry and fears, a lifetime in advance, that only a parent of a child with additional needs understands. And whatever about the availability of services for children in Ireland living with autism, adult services are virtually non-existent based on my knowledge and insight.

I've also felt feelings of embarrassment, which I hate myself for. When we've been at a park or in a shopping centre and my child is screaming, kicking me, or pulling things off the shelves, I've felt a bit embarrassed. Then I feel guilt for feeling embarrassed! Autism is often a hidden disability, so other people can't see the internal processes and issues happening for the child in that moment. You may feel like a bad parent, or that other people think that of you.

I questioned if I was a good enough parent to do this: to care for my child and meet all their needs. On particularly difficult and challenging days I have felt I wasn't good enough, or strong enough, or resilient enough, to cope.

Some parents feel intense anger when their child is diagnosed as autistic. You may feel that this is so unfair, you want your child not to have to struggle in their lives socially or emotionally. You may feel angry at the system, the waiting lists for assessments, or the lack of resources and services available to help your child. Anger can also cause conflict between parents. I've spoken to many parents whose spouse or family members don't accept the diagnosis of autism and feel that one parent is actively seeking a diagnosis. So there can be some blame attributed in these situations.

Basically, you can feel so many different emotions on your journey to discovering your child is autistic and may revisit all of these throughout your journey. But each and every emotion you feel is valid. You feel however you feel. Allow yourself this time. Take your time in processing and adjusting to how you feel and try not to feel guilty for this. It can be a lonely time too with all of these emotions. No one else may understand exactly how you feel in these moments. Even your partner may feel differently and it can be tough to cope with the weight of your emotions throughout the process.

How can you process your emotions and feelings around your child's autism?

As I was processing all of these emotions with each of my children on their journeys, I tried my best not to let them feel the effects of this. It's not easy, but it's important that we try to shield our children from the adult emotions regarding their diagnosis and to not project these feelings unintentionally on to our child. If your child thinks you feel sad or shocked at their diagnosis, then they might think that's how they should feel. They could develop negative feelings towards themselves and autism. So until you feel in a place where you have processed your child's diagnosis and the feelings you have around this, you should limit the depth of conversation you have with your child about this. Our children are very bright and intuitive little creatures and they pick up on a lot more than we may realise, particularly regarding our feelings and emotions. Sharing your child's diagnosis with them is covered in more detail in Chapter 4.

Talking with a professional counsellor is a really great way to process your emotions in coming to terms with an autism diagnosis for your child. I really believe in counselling and have found it to be an important aspect in my life that helps me to keep going when things get really tough. My counsellor is someone completely outside of my circle of family and friends whom I can share my most raw feelings with. As parents we often never verbalise some of our fears or worries about our kids. Counselling is a place where I can offload all of the emotions I have been carrying and maybe not processing. I literally feel lighter leaving the place and like I can start again on a clean slate with my feelings and coping capacity. Counsellors are non-judgemental and will really, really listen to all of your concerns. They don't offer specific advice, but they do help you to understand and let go of some of the feelings you have that might be weighing you down and preventing you from moving forward and being the best parent you can be. The 'mom guilt' I carried (and still carry!) is heavy enough to stick me to the ground at times. Counselling has helped immensely with this. I also feel that attending counselling was for my children too. If I try my best to look after my mind and my well-being, I am more in a position to be the best mom I can be for my children.

Support groups (either in person or online) can help you to work through your feelings around your child's diagnosis, and also to gain more certainty about what to expect. No one else knows exactly how you feel, but other parents further down the road can certainly empathise and are an amazing source of support. You can also ask the healthcare professional who is assessing your child for support. They may be able to provide a space to listen to your concerns or worries, or may direct you to another service that can help. But having an avenue to express your emotions while processing a diagnosis is a must.

Focusing on today and tomorrow, as opposed to next week or next year, is some of the best advice I've ever been given. I used to lie awake at night and think of the worst-case scenario in my head about my children and their needs. I used to worry sick about what might happen in school, how they might feel if 'x' happened or if 'y' happened. Slowly (very slowly) I managed to help myself not think about these things. I ask myself instead: 'Is thinking about this going to benefit my child? Or benefit me or my family?' If the answer is 'No', I don't let the thought in. Or, if I'm worrying about one of my children, for example something relating to whether they will be able to live independently, I now think of ways to increase the likelihood of this happening, as opposed to worrying that it won't. So I'll look at skills building, developing independence and slowly supporting my children to do more for themselves. I haven't reduced my fears or my worries, but I have reduced how much space I give them in my head. Only I can choose what thoughts I let into my mind. It's a tough skill to learn, but it is possible to develop this skill for yourself.

What the experts say

When you receive the news that your child is autistic, this makes you as a parent feel concern for them for the rest of their lives. Ordinarily we imagine guiding and caring for our children until they reach adulthood. But autism means that we will potentially need us to care for them when they reach adulthood. Abbott, Bernard and Forge[35] suggest that considering the lifelong impact autism will have on their child's life can be particularly challenging for parents.

Parental reactions to a diagnosis of autism for their child are varied according to Rasmussen and colleagues.[36] They propose that parents can feel relief, sadness, guilt, or all of these combined. Anderberg and South[37] suggest that parents' thoughts and expectations prior to assessment and diagnosis impact how they cope with their child's eventual diagnosis. Parents who have read up on autism and strongly suspect their child has autism, tend to adjust to the diagnosis more easily.[37] Hence parents who don't suspect autism or know little about the condition may struggle more with processing the news that their child is autistic. Gentles and colleagues suggest that parents who strongly suspect their child is autistic tend to cope better when they receive an official diagnosis compared to parents who are unsure or who don't think their child is autistic. And parents who already had a child diagnosed with autism were less shocked or surprised when a subsequent child was diagnosed.[38]

Most worries and fears at the time of your child's autism diagnosis stem from the sense of uncertainty presented by this.[39] Equally, many parents worry about the negative stereotypes around autism and the stigma presented by this.[40] Jacobs and colleagues in 2020 found that fears surrounding how their child would be treated were a further common concern for parents. Courcy and Des Rivières-Pigeon in their 2021 study, report that many parents find the advice and support they need from other parents of autistic children that they connect with. Some families expressed a reduction in their interactions and supports from their own families due to the stigma surrounding autism and behaviours their children might exhibit.[41]

Guilt is another common documented emotion felt by parents upon learning of their child's autism diagnosis.[42] Lopez and colleagues report that mothers often question if they have done something to cause their child to be autistic and feel responsible for their child's diagnosis.[42] Feelings of guilt were found in 81% of parents interviewed by Kuhn and Carter, in light of their child's autism diagnosis. This study further suggests that parents, and mothers in particular, may question their parental competence because of this guilt they feel.[43] Kuhn and Carter further highlight the importance of supporting parental well-being, to improve parents' feelings of competence in their parenting ability.[43]

Some parents can feel immense relief with the diagnosis of autism.[35] Rasmussen and colleagues describe feelings of relief enabling parents to better understand the reasoning behind their child's difficulties and perhaps the realisation that these difficulties were not because of bad parenting.[36] This is really interesting and something that really resonates with me. I felt relief in knowing that there was an explanation for aggressive and violent behaviour, and in understanding more why traditional parenting approaches to responding to this didn't work. I suppose I kind of felt vindicated, if this makes sense? Also, parents feel relief as they now have a new set of ideas and strategies to help their child which are specific to an autism diagnosis and the understanding which comes with this.[36]

Potter in 2017 conducted a study concerning fathers' experiences relating to their child's diagnosis of autism as this is largely underreported.[44] Potter found that fathers sometimes felt denial when initially receiving a diagnosis and noted that this can cause a strain within their relationship with the other parent.[44] This is certainly true from my experiences with talking to other parents. Some parents are so deeply upset that they refuse to accept the diagnosis of autism and can remain in denial even after the diagnosis is confirmed.

Another study into parents' reactions to their child's diagnosis of autism found that the severity of the autism and the symptoms of this impacts a parent's ability to accept the diagnosis.[45] Parents of children with more significant care needs may find the diagnosis more challenging to process as they continue to meet their child's care needs every day while coping with their own emotions.[45]

Da Paz and colleagues[46] argue that parental acceptance of their child's diagnosis reduces the stress and despair that comes with this. The more accepting the parent is of the diagnosis, the less this will negatively affect them emotionally. Murphy and Tierney[47] suggest that parents' experiences of the whole process of assessment and diagnosis and managing their child's needs without a diagnosis or intervention to date, further impacts how they cope with and adjust to their child's autism diagnosis.

Some parents experience a sort of grieving process when they receive their child's diagnosis. They feel the loss of the life they expected for their child and the milestones they would meet, compared to the reality that autism may change their potential pathways into adult life.[38] Grieving is very much a normal element of processing a diagnosis of autism for your child and shouldn't be something you feel guilty about. According to Bravo-Benítez and colleagues,[48] parents may feel a cycle of grief as emotions fluctuate and they try to understand what the future holds for their child. Uncertainty about the future and accepting a future which contrasts with the one you had imagined, contributes to prolonged feelings of loss at this time.[48] Grief is also related to things you can't do as a family such as perhaps going grocery shopping, swimming or to social events with your child, depending on their needs.[48] For example, if we are having a really tough day and one of my children is really struggling, sometimes we cancel events we planned to attend. If my child is completely overwhelmed, I don't want to place them in situations which will make this even harder for them. So we do miss some events and activities because of this.

O'Brien[49] describes the grief some parents experience at the time of diagnosis as an 'ambiguous loss'. Ambiguous loss is defined by Boss[50] as an incomplete or unclear loss, a loss without an ending, and a loss of perhaps a part of someone, while that someone is still with you. Boss describes ambiguous loss as ongoing and something you live with. O'Brien found that parents experience ambiguous loss concerning their autistic child as they appear and are healthy physically, but they struggle substantially behaviourally or socially. Equally, the uncertainty of everyday and what that day might bring in terms of coping or challenging behaviour, further contribute to the ambiguity concerning the sadness parents feel.[49] For example, I have felt this loss when I see my children's peers maybe passing them out socially, being more mature or more capable, or perhaps conforming more to social norms such as going places on their own, or arranging to meet friends. I feel this as a loss sometimes. I feel sad that my child can't do this, and sad that maybe they never will.

Some parents may search non-stop for information on autism as they attempt to adjust to their child's diagnosis, while other parents may avoid this information as they cope with the feelings a diagnosis can bring.[47] I think this is very much an individual reaction. I find that if I have all of (or a lot of) the information, I can mentally prepare for what might happen. Whereas my husband would argue that this creates much more worry about the 'what ifs' and would rather take things as they come, and react as needed.

Fear and worry for the future are also more likely for parents of children with disabilities, and this is impacted by the ambiguity and uncertainty about what the future holds.[51] Bujnowska and colleagues report that mothers in particular experience future anxiety, and worry about their own health and the detrimental effect that a major health episode could have on their ability to care for their child.[51]

McCabe reports that parent-to-parent support is really beneficial in helping parents to cope with their fears and worries, following their child's autism diagnosis.[52] Speaking to parents who are in a similar position can further result in getting more insights about methods of supporting your child, which they found successful with theirs.[52] In fact, parents sometimes find informal supports more helpful than formal supports in reducing stress levels and improving their emotional wellbeing.[53] Shepherd and colleagues propose that informal supports accessed through social media are more accessible to most parents. While 45% of the parents who participated in their study found social media support from other parents of autistic children beneficial.[53]

In summary, the research suggests that parents' fears and worries throughout the diagnostic process for their child vary substantially. Parents can feel guilt, sadness, loss, fear for the future or relief, or may feel a combination of all of these emotions, or go back and forth between them. The bottom line is ... it's tough. Adjusting to your new reality as a parent of an autistic child is tough emotionally. It's often the first step into the unknown and the uncertainty about the future can be really upsetting and confusing. Take your time. Process your emotions and get as much information as you need, as you begin to accept and adjust to your child's diagnosis.

KEY LEARNING POINTS FROM THIS CHAPTER:

- Take your time to process your own emotions regarding your child's diagnosis.
- Ask for help and support from family and consider counselling.
- Feelings of guilt, sadness, grief, loss and relief are common and completely normal.
- You and your child's other parent may react completely differently to your child's diagnosis and this is okay.
- Many parents fear for their child's future and worry about what might happen if they become unable to care for their child, or what will happen when the parents die.
- Your understanding and ideas about autism prior to diagnosis will impact how you react to this.
- The stigma surrounding autism can further create worry for parents as they fear how their child will be treated as a result of their diagnosis.
- Accessing more information about autism and how you can best help and support your child can help you to accept their diagnosis and have a clearer plan for the future.
- Other parents of autistic children can offer helpful guidance and support.

Conclusion

This chapter explored some of the common fears and worries that parents might feel when they receive the news that their child is autistic. Your concerns about your child are valid and also an expression of how much you love them and want the best for them. Taking the time to process your own emotions and fears prior to supporting your child to process their own diagnosis is important. If you have accepted the diagnosis, you will be calmer and more able to support your child to accept this too. Feelings like guilt, grief, relief, anger and sadness are common when your child is diagnosed as autistic. You are re-adjusting your expectations of how you thought your family life would be and this can take time. None of these feelings are wrong. Breathe, get more information and connect with other parents of autistic children for advice and support. You've got this!

4

TELLING YOUR CHILD THEY ARE AUTISTIC

Introduction

This is one of the questions I am asked most frequently: when should you tell your child they are autistic? I know much of what I know now from previous mistakes. But I also realise that each journey through autism is different and each child is different. However, I wholeheartedly feel that telling your child they have autism at the earliest possible opportunity is the best option. This can be more challenging if you yourself are struggling with the emotions presented by your child's diagnosis, or can be more difficult if your child is having substantial emotional or behavioural issues.

This chapter will explore my experiences of telling each of my three children that they had autism. The first time was pretty traumatic, while the second and third time were very uneventful. Ways of gently introducing the idea of autism within your family will be discussed. This chapter will further present a review of what the experts say about telling your child they are autistic.

My experiences

First time around Ellie was referred to the mental health team at age three with challenging behaviour. We attended regular sessions with psychology, occupational therapy, psychiatry, social care groups for developing social skills, family therapy, cognitive behavioural therapy and clinical nurse specialists. As mentioned previously, Ellie's initial diagnosis was ODD at age four. Then she was diagnosed with ADHD at age seven. Finally, Ellie was diagnosed with autism at age eleven. Ellie had so many assessments we lost count, in-school observations, educational assessments, ADHD assessments and autism assessments. But for a long time she didn't quite fit all the criteria for autism so this is why her diagnosis was so late. Ellie was on three different medications until we found what worked. She hated going to appointments but accepted this was part of her life. She didn't know anything different.

One day coming back from an appointment when she was fourteen, I mentioned something about autism. Ellie looked at me with a shocked expression and said: 'But I don't have autism?' I was completely shocked. I said: 'Yes you do, love.' She screamed and cried and asked me again if she really had autism. She looked as though I had knocked the wind out of her. She cried for hours. She was shocked, horrified, embarrassed and angry. Angry that she had autism and angry that I didn't tell her. Everything whirred around in my head like a whirlwind. Ellie was with us at every appointment, attended the autism social skills groups, had a special needs assistant throughout primary and secondary school. So I thought she knew. But I had never directly said those words: 'Ellie, you have autism.' I assumed Ellie knew ... she had to know, or so I thought. But she did not know. I felt like I had shattered her whole world in that moment.

It took months before Ellie was able to talk about it. The mention of the 'a' word sent her into an emotional outburst. Slowly over the next two years, Ellie was able to talk about having autism. Understanding autism helped Ellie to understand herself better and some of the challenges she had. The best description of autism we were given was by a psychiatrist who said: 'Picture yourself being dropped alone into the middle of the busiest street in Beijing. Picture standing there in an unfamiliar place ... with people who all look different, who all speak a different language, who can see how different you are. Imagine the noise, the strange smells and the sense of panic you might feel. Well this is how autistic people feel every day.'

This was such a practical and insightful explanation and Ellie agreed that this was how she felt sometimes. In school, on the bus, in strange or new situations. Another way autism was described by my littlest love, Daisy, was through explaining that her brain is like playdough. But her playdough is white, and she doesn't like mixing playdough because you can't get back to the original colour. Daisy said that when she goes to school and everyone is talking and moving that they all have different colour playdough and they are trying to mix with hers and she doesn't want this to happen. This was another really good visual description of what autism feels like, from the mind of a seven-year-old.

Fast forward and here we are with Alex and he is ten years old. We'd finally twigged that there may be more to Alex's needs than dyspraxia. I can't understand how we didn't see it before now! And now that one cog clicked into place, each cog followed suit and everything makes much more sense. So, at this point we started talking about autism every day. We began by talking about how all people are different and all have different abilities. We explained that Ellie is autistic and that this means some things might be harder for her, such as school or noisy places. We talked about how some autistic people have amazing talents and usually find themselves being an expert in some subjects. Over the next few months we talked about autism more frequently and it became our norm. We then explained to Alex that he may have autism and we were going to be meeting some doctors to find out. He asked a few questions such as: 'Why did we think he might have autism?' And: 'How will we know for sure?' I answered honestly, explaining that Alex found changes very tough like when we moved the furniture around, or when we got a new car. I explained that when he was unsure what to do sometimes, he might shut down or become upset. I told Alex we would be meeting with doctors and doing some quizzes, and that teacher and I would also answer some questions. Alex seemed happy enough with this and didn't ask any other questions. I would discuss autism regularly to help Alex to understand himself more. For example, if he was finding his socks or clothes uncomfortable, I would explain what sensory issues are and that sometimes autistic people experience this. Or if he was struggling with a change in the school timetable, I would say I know this is very hard for you and that autism can make coping with changes extra tough, so it's okay to be upset.

When we started Alex's autism assessment, we spoke about autism even more regularly. Alex became more inquisitive and was quite intrigued by the assessment process too. So the day I got the call to confirm Alex's autism diagnosis, I told him immediately. It was a non-event. He asked if I was sure, and exactly what the doctor had said. And that was it. He didn't ask any additional questions and accepted that now we knew for sure. The build-up to suspecting autism and sharing this with Alex certainly made sharing the eventual diagnosis with him much easier. He anticipated and expected this so there was no shock. And having given him information gradually, this helped him to accept the possibility initially and then the eventual confirmation.

So at this point, two of my three children have autism or suspected autism, so I'm practically an expert right? You would think that. Well it wasn't the case. Miss Daisy, Daisy, my youngest, was displaying some challenging behaviours and we went through the usual referral process. I thought maybe she might have ADHD. But Daisy's needs were very different from Ellie's and Alex's. Yet at our first meeting with the paediatrician she explained that she suspected Daisy was autistic. I was shocked. We told Daisy straight away (at age six) that she might be autistic. We answered questions and explained the assessment process.

Daisy was like a duck taking to water and when her eventual diagnosis was confirmed a year later, she was actually delighted. She screamed: 'Yay I have autism, I have autism!' She wanted to be just like her big sister Ellie and loved that she was different. Daisy felt celebration and pride at her diagnosis, which was so beautiful to see. The diagnosis also helped Daisy to understand why clothing really upset her, or why she became so worried with new social situations. We went for the official in-person diagnosis with Daisy and the professionals painted a really positive, unique and special picture of Daisy being autistic, and this further cemented the positive view she had about her diagnosis and about herself. It was such a contrast to our experience with Ellie. But so much had changed. It was eight years later and we as a society have evolved considerably in our understanding of autism in this time. And as Daisy's difficulties were less severe or life-disrupting than Ellie's, it meant that perhaps the diagnosis was clearer to see.

But all of my children's very different journeys to an autism diagnosis highlight that discussing autism prior to assessment and eventual diagnosis is the best way to help your child to adjust when a diagnosis is made. Alternatively, as early as possible after a diagnosis is made, you should start working towards telling your child they are autistic. I think talking generally about autism first, maybe watching some YouTube clips or reading some age-appropriate books on autism can be a great way to pave the way towards telling your child about their diagnosis. You need to normalise autism so that your child doesn't see this as a deficit or something that's wrong with them but more of an addition to their personality and something that makes them unique. Speaking positively about autism, perhaps identifying positive autistic role models and creating a space for your child to ask any question they want to, will further help you both with processing an eventual diagnosis.

Finally, have your own ducks in a row before you share with your child! Your feelings, worries and emotions are very valid, and you should take time to process these. If you are upset or anxious about your child's diagnosis, they may feel this and share these feelings of worry or upset. So take your time and ensure you yourself have accepted the diagnosis. And try to be calm, open and reassuring when your child asks questions. You can also use books to help both you and your child to understand more about autism and what this means. We did get a book for Alex about famous autistic people in the hope that this would help him to feel more positive about his diagnosis. He threw it under his bed and asked me daily for the next five weeks why I bought him this book and said that he didn't want it. But I wouldn't have known this unless I tried. We both learned that this approach didn't work for Alex. But Daisy might be delighted to get the same book.

Equally, professionals, from those who completed my children's assessments, to therapy providers and all school staff (teachers, resource teachers and SNAs), have all supported us with the process of helping our children to accept and understand their diagnosis of autism. In particular, when we went to get Daisy's diagnosis, the paediatrician and psychologist spoke to Daisy about her amazing superpowers of autism, and how she was unique, special and wonderful. They spoke so positively and with such animation that

Daisy was delighted with herself. She was beaming with pride and did indeed feel very special. This highlighted to me the significance of the way the news of the diagnosis is delivered to your child. If you are positive and hopeful when you share your child's diagnosis with them, this is what they will remember and these are the feelings and emotions you are projecting to them. This is why I have written a chapter on processing your own fears and worries prior to sharing your child's diagnosis with them. Children don't need our worries or our distress, they need our belief and our unwavering love and support. So make sure for you, emotionally, that the time is right for you to deliver the news of your child's diagnosis. But also know that not one of us is perfect. My own experiences in this chapter (and in the rest of this book!) highlight just that. Do your best, that's all you can do.

What do the experts tell us about when to tell children they are autistic?

Very little research to date has been undertaken to find out about parents' and children's experiences of telling a child they are autistic.[54] I really struggled with finding literature on this topic for this chapter. However, the resounding feedback from most autistic adults online is that telling a child they are autistic at the earliest possible opportunity is best.

Crane and colleagues in 2019 had 558 parents of autistic children participate in their research, and found that 7% of the parents said they 'thought' their child knew about their diagnosis, while 24% of parents said their child did not know they were autistic.[54] However, Pike notes that many autistic adults express a wish that they had been told about their diagnosis earlier, and that children have a right to know that they are autistic.[55]

The American Academy of Paediatrics advise telling your child they have been diagnosed with autism in a safe and calm environment where they have an opportunity to ask questions and express how they feel.[56] Some autistic children identify themselves as different to their peers due to having a special needs assistant in school, or attending therapy appointments. It's important that your child finds out about their autism diagnosis from you, as opposed to accidentally in school or at an appointment where other adults assume your child knows already.[56]

The Centre for Autism Research (CAR) advise that when to tell your child they are autistic should depend on their age and level of understanding.[57] Additional challenges can occur when a child is older and perhaps in their teens and they have a high level of cognitive functioning.[57] This can cause a great deal of shock and upset as the young person may feel a loss of understanding of their own identity and the emotional difficulties associated with this. Dundon suggests that it's important for parents themselves to be ready and to have processed their own feelings prior to sharing their diagnosis with their child.[58] Many parents feel sadness, grief, guilt, frustration and fear when they learn their child is autistic. Telling your child while still processing these emotions yourself would not be helpful to them. You need to be calm, confident and clear when you talk to your child about their autism and to be in a position to cope with and respond to their emotions.

Some parents delay telling their child about their diagnosis as they feel they are protecting them.[59] Wishing family life would go back to how it was previously is another reason some parents don't tell their child immediately when they have been diagnosed with autism.[59] Jones argues that children may experience an increase in self-esteem when they are told about their diagnosis.[60] Oftentimes, high-functioning autistic children may be aware that they are different and a diagnosis can help them to understand more about themselves. Huws and Jones interviewed autistic young people for their study and participants who experienced a delay in being told about their autism felt this affected them negatively.[61] Participants reported that it was harder to accept their diagnosis if time had lapsed from when their parents found out about their diagnosis until they told them.

Wheeler suggests that although it's difficult to know the right time to tell your child they have been diagnosed with autism, delaying telling them is more likely to result in increased distress for them.[62] Approaching the conversation with a positive and upbeat tone will communicate to your child how you feel about their diagnosis. Wheeler further proposes that in the case of your family, you may feel that a medical professional should tell your child about their autism diagnosis and you can be in the room or nearby. Every family is different and you can only do what you think is best for your family and your child.

Foden suggests that your child's age and understanding will further inform your decision about when to tell them they are autistic.[63] If your child is six or seven but pre-verbal, you may choose to wait and introduce their diagnosis more gradually. Whereas if your child is fourteen and is attending a mainstream school when they receive a diagnosis, telling them immediately may be more appropriate. Professionals involved in the process of diagnosis or who provide services to your child can also help and support you to tell your child about their diagnosis.[55]

Should you tell other people about your child's autism?

Again the answer to this should be based on your child and their unique needs. Ellie has had so many meltdowns because I've told people and has said that this is her story to tell, and not mine. This is a fair and valid point. But what was harder to explain to Ellie is that other people may react negatively to her and her needs when they don't know. Often when people do know they are more under-standing and welcoming. For example, at events Ellie may punch another child for what seems like no reason. Or she could scream, kick, bite or run away from an event. The stares of other people at a time like this make these very challenging situations even harder. I found that by explaining Ellie was autistic, people stared less and we could work through the outburst and the feelings associated with this more quickly without other people making her feel even more uncomfortable. Equally, when Ellie hurt another child, it was important for other parents and the child to know that Ellie had autism and perhaps misinterpreted some communication, or became overwhelmed. Now this is by no means an excuse. Actions have consequences and whenever another person is hurt by my child, there has to be a consequence. But telling other parents meant they were often more understanding and less likely to withdraw their child from future playdates or activities and this would potentially make Ellie feel less excluded than she might have felt otherwise. And I am equally conscious that our autistic children often don't notice their own behaviours which may cause distress to other people. Misinterpreting their own behaviours and those of other people is common for our children.

Yet some autistic children may have greater needs, socially, emotionally and physically. If a child is unable to function socially or is presented with very distressing feelings when trying to, it is important that other people are made aware of this. This is to ease the potential stress felt by the child (perhaps by reducing noise, not standing so close) and also to reduce the potential negative reaction to the child from other people. For example, if your child is having a meltdown in a restaurant, people are often more understanding when they know your child has additional needs.

You can tell people verbally, or you can use a cue card explaining your child's additional needs. This could be a small laminated card which says that your child has autism and may have difficulties in social situations. Equally, now that Ellie is an adult, it is totally her decision whether or not to tell people that she's autistic. She has managed to avoid situations which she will find uncomfortable and is better able to cope when she does feel uncomfortable than when she was a child. She doesn't tell very many people that she's autistic and fears the stigma surrounding this may impact how she is viewed. And unfortunately, this does happen.

KEY LEARNING POINTS FROM THIS CHAPTER:

- Allow yourself enough time to process your own feelings and come to terms with your child's autism diagnosis before you tell them. Our children are sponges and they soak up many unspoken feelings. If you feel anxious, sad or stressed when you share their diagnosis with them, it could result in them feeling this way too.
- Research autism yourself. There's a lot of information online and there are useful videos on YouTube. Connect with other parents of children on the spectrum. These are your people and they understand all the emotions you feel now and your fears and worries for the future. Online support groups are very accessible and some of the best tips I've gotten have come from other moms.
- Find information to share with your child after you tell them about their autism diagnosis. This could be a book suitable for their age,

or a video online, or a fact sheet for children. Allow your child time to process what you have told them and as they ask questions you can slowly begin sharing more information with them.

- Some children and teens will not want any more information and may not want to acknowledge or talk about their diagnosis. This is completely okay. We can only respond to the individual needs of our own child, and there's no one right way to parent an autistic child.
- Choose a good time and an appropriate environment for when you will first discuss your child's diagnosis with them.
- Be positive when discussing autism with your child or in general. A positive mindset and approach will help your child to view autism and themself in a more positive way.
- Normalise autism and discuss it in your home with your children, whether or not they have autism.
- Ask your child if they want you to share this information with other people. Explain how this may help them and help other people to be more understanding of their needs.
- Try to pre-empt and plan for what questions your child might ask and how you might answer these. You won't have all the answers, but reassuring your child that no matter what happens you will be there with them is very important.

Conclusion

This chapter discussed the opportunities and challenges presented regarding when and how to tell your child they have been diagnosed with autism. My three experiences with my own autistic children were so different. But my experience of waiting with Ellie, and assuming she knew, turned out not to be a good decision for her at all, and I will carry the guilt of this memory with me forever. However, the age of your child, their level of understanding, and your own coping capacity and family support network will all play a part in your decision about when to tell your child they are autistic. I believe, based on my experiences, that speaking about autism regularly and normalising this normal part of your family, prior to telling your child about their diagnosis, definitely helps your child to digest and accept this information. Do prioritise planning to tell your child they are autistic. The earlier your child knows about their diagnosis, the more time they will have to process this and adjust to it. It's a part of who they are and their identity, so speaking about autism positively to your child is really important.

5

AUTISM AND OTHER PEOPLE

Introduction

It's one thing going through the process of an autism diagnosis with your child, and then accepting this yourself as a parent. Then supporting your child to cope with their own diagnosis can be another really challenging time. But one of the most difficult and unnecessary challenges within this period is, by far, coping with the responses of well-meaning family and friends. It is so disheartening and upsetting when you feel judged as a parent, or you feel that your child is being judged. This adds to the stress, worry and frustration families may feel at the time of diagnosis, and the words of family members can stay with you. Equally challenging is the unhelpful judgement, staring or comments from people in public places regarding your child's behavioural or emotional needs.

This chapter will discuss what not to say to the parents of an autistic child and is specifically aimed at (and addresses) family members and friends. I will discuss and explore how you can best support your family member or friend if their child is autistic. I will share my many and varied experiences of being given unsolicited 'advice' on parenting and will discuss some of the other not-so-helpful things I've been told about autism. This chapter will explore what you can say and do to be helpful and will further give guidance on how to respond supportively when a diagnosis of autism is shared with you. The views of experts will be explored in an attempt to understand why people react the way they do, as parents, friends and family members of an autistic child. Finally, this chapter will provide key learning points and tips on how you can best support your loved one and their child on their autism journey.

My experiences

I've had friends and family members advise me on my parenting (and often in front of my children), or attempt to intervene without being asked to when I am responding to my children's needs. This absolutely comes from a place of love, care and a wish to help. But it is usually not helpful and actually contributes to increased stress levels and a feeling of being judged. Equally, I've had family/friends who have just put their arms out to give me the biggest hug, or who take the extra time to find out more about my child and how they can help them on their journey by changing little things to make life easier for them. The most helpful comments are ones that express an openness to autism, what this is and what this means for my child. Or questions are also very much appreciated. When someone asks lots of questions, this communicates to me that they are curious and care enough to ask. However, a big bold list of what not to say is still super helpful! I've provided this list to give a realistic insight into what you think may be a helpful or appropriate comment, but which can actually be really hurtful. I've likely said some of these things myself, before realising how they are received. And I have the most loving and caring circle of family and friends who have said these things to me with absolutely no intention to cause upset. But I think naming these things outright will be helpful to raise awareness of their potential impact on a parent who might feel close to the edge of their coping capacity.

Below is a list which illustrates what NOT to say (this list is not exhaustive!):

Figure 5.1: What not to say to a parent after an autism diagnosis

- Sure everyone has autism these days.
- There was no such thing as autism years ago.
- He's just different.
- They can't know for sure though that it's autism?

- Labelling your child is damaging.
- Everyone is diagnosed with something now.
- Autism is being over-diagnosed.
- I just don't see it.

- She seems perfectly normal to me.
- Maybe she'll grow out of it.
- A lot of parents are looking for excuses for their child's behaviour and look for diagnoses.

- I don't think he has autism.
- If it was autism she wouldn't be able to sit in school all day.
- He made eye contact with me the other day, so it can't be autism.
- It's just a label.

- Sure I have autism myself.
- Are you sure?
- But it must be only mild autism?
- Well my neighbour's child has autism and her needs are severe.

I've heard each of these responses when I have shared with my nearest and dearest about each of my children's diagnoses of autism. None of these were helpful and many made me feel judged, like I was actively seeking a diagnosis for God knows what reason, or that I was misinterpreting my child's needs or making excuses for bad behaviours. What I wanted to scream from the top of my voice was:

- Autism diagnoses take considerable time. You don't go in on a Monday with concerns and by Friday have a diagnosis.
- The criteria for an autism diagnosis are extremely specific and issues must be present across settings (school, home, crèche, etc.) for a diagnosis to be made.
- Two professionals assessed each of my children independently, and only when both agreed was a diagnosis made.
- The diagnostic process is comprehensive and robust and involves observation in school, a detailed survey of both parent

and teacher experiences with the child, direct assessment with the child and discussion with a multidisciplinary team.

- No one wants or seeks an autism diagnosis for their child. I wish my child didn't have to cope with the challenges autism brings to their lives. I wish they didn't struggle every day with tasks other children fly through.
- I have yet to meet or hear of a person who was misdiagnosed with autism, likely due to the multi-element assessment and comprehensive diagnostic process.
- It was already really tough parenting an autistic child and seeing them distressed, upset or unable to cope. I really need my family and friends to be supportive.
- You don't have to respond! I'm not telling you for your take on this, or validation, or agreement.
- Say nothing if you don't know what to say. I'd prefer someone to say 'I don't know how to respond', or to ask how they could help, rather than say something unhelpful.

Sometimes responses or questions are funny and we can't help but respond with humour. If someone makes a face or stares at one of my children, I have said: 'Be careful, it's highly contagious' (in the most serious voice possible). Ellie wins the award though for the best reply. Recently, a friend who we hadn't seen for years said to her: 'Sure you don't have autism?' Ellie said: 'I do yeah, it's here in my back pocket, I keep it hidden.' It was comical! The poor guy didn't know where to look. But he was being honest and he was curious, so it's completely okay that he asked the question.

What do we, as parents, need from you, as family members and friends? We need you to accept our children, to do things that will help not hinder our children, and we need you to be a listening ear and supportive when we, as parents, are struggling.

So what does accepting our children look like for family members? For me, when our family doesn't bat an eyelid to stimming, this communicates the most loving acceptance of my children. If Daisy is screaming when I'm putting on her shoes or Alex is rocking while we're out somewhere, family and friends understanding this as their normal and completely okay, is really helpful. So not questioning stimming, not intervening if challenging behaviour arises (without asking), and not passing comment on our response as parents to our child's needs helps. Other people and especially in public, see only a tiny snippet of your child's needs and have no insight into their day so far, or what they might be trying to communicate. For example, if you visit and Daisy is screaming, throwing things down the stairs and hits me. This may be the tail end of a two-hour meltdown, this may be because she's in pain or unwell and isn't able to communicate this. Or this could be happening because she's worried about school the next day or an event coming up. It's always more than the behaviour and it's always more than that moment you witness. Sometimes silence is the best form of support for parents, rather than feeling the need to give an opinion or advice.

Being unhelpful would be arranging a visit, playdate or outing with my child and arriving late (or early), or changing plans at the last minute. Equally, spur-of-the-moment plans don't work for many autistic children. If someone calls and says: 'We're on our way, we will take Daisy to the park ...' Daisy ends up hysterical as she has had no time to prepare for this. Or if relatives are coming over for lunch and are an hour late, Alex will sit at the window from about half an hour beforehand and will ask every five minutes what the time is and how many minutes until they arrive. Then after the time has passed he will repeat over and over again that they were meant to be here at 2.00 p.m., but they are not here. He will want to know why and will continue to become increasingly frustrated until we have certainty again about when they will come and what will happen. Our children need reliability, they need reassurance and they need to know what to expect. Please do remember this. The annoyance of being late for you, could be extremely distressing for them.

What should family members and friends say?

It's sometimes hard to say anything, especially if you are afraid of saying the wrong thing or putting your foot in it. But it is a good idea to just listen sometimes. Often parents need a support person, who is a family member or close friend, so they can offload when things are tough. It is equally important to remember that parents love their child so much and with all of their heart, regardless of autism or challenging behaviour. Acknowledging this is always welcome and helpful. Some general things you can say around an autism diagnosis are outlined below.

Ask questions, ask what this means for the child and ask if you can do anything to help or support the family. Ask the parent how they feel, or how their child feels about their diagnosis. Ask the parent what you could do if their child becomes distressed or agitated in order to help. Or ask what the parent needs most right now to cope with their child's needs and perhaps their own emotions or worries. More than anything, just be there. You don't have to say anything. Just be there with them and for them.

What do the experts say?

Stigma can substantially and negatively impact the families of children living with autism.[64] Lodder and colleagues argue that parents can feel blame and responsibility for their child's behaviour or any difficulties they experience, particularly in public.[64] Parents have historically been blamed for causing autism, according to Neely-Barnes and colleagues.[65] Another research study found that parents experienced blame for their child's autism from extended family members.[66] The invisibility of autism can further exacerbate judgement and stigma, as people only see the behaviour and perhaps don't consider the potential cause.[65]

Gray reports that parents have experienced staring, unhelpful and judgemental comments, and avoidance from other people.[67] How the parent interprets such stigma can further increase social exclusion and bring more negative impacts of stigma on the whole family. For example, if I'm feeling strong and feel like I'm coping well, I can let perceived stigma roll off my back and not bother me. But on a day I'm maybe not feeling the best, or after a challenging few days with one of the children, stigma can really hurt and even result in us not attending an event (because of how I worry my children will be treated or judged). So stigma for some families can be pretty devastating. I meet a lot of moms online who no longer leave their house except for the school run. The stares, smart comments and whispers have resulted in them deciding that any benefit of leaving the house is just not worth the upset for them or their child. Some parents also avoid interactions with family members and friends for this same reason.

The severity of the difficulties the child experiences can increase the negative impact of stigma on the child and their family.[68] Research with families of autistic children further suggests that stigma can result in exclusion and rejection of the child socially, and this further creates worry and stress for parents.[68] Therefore, children with more profound difficulties arising from their autism diagnosis or those with the greatest additional needs could be even more negatively affected by stigma.

A really interesting study completed in Hong Kong reports that the perceived control other people think the child has over their behaviour and actions can impact how they respond.[69] If people think a child is intentionally misbehaving or being disruptive, they are more likely to feel irritation or anger towards the child. In contrast, if the person thinks the child is not in control of their own behaviour and it's due to their condition, they are more likely to be sympathetic and kind in their responses. This reiterates why I've felt the need to share my children's diagnoses with other people, in the hope of prompting a better understanding of their needs and acceptability of their behaviours.

Anticipated stigma is when parents fear how their child will be treated because of the negative stereotypes surrounding autism.[70] Quinn and Earnshaw suggest that we can expect less fair treatment or rejection based on what we think or worry that other people think, or by how we perceive that they view our child.[70] This is certainly something I can relate to. I can feel myself almost bracing for impact when attending certain events with my children. I almost expect judgement or exclusion for my children in advance. It's not that I accept this, but I think I mentally prepare myself for this so that it's not as upsetting when it happens (which it does). For example, the stares at the park if my child is screaming, or the expected response if my child doesn't quite 'fit in' during a group activity (like the school play or at a family party). It's probably a method of self-protection, but it's most definitely rooted in stigma. Even to the extent where I wonder if we don't get invited to other people's homes sometimes, because of my children's additional needs.

Increasing awareness about autism can help to reduce stigma for children and their families. I do find myself (even now) often explaining to family members what autism is and how this impacts my children in every aspect of their lives. I suppose I'm constantly advocating for my children to be accepted just as they are. We 'do' autism in our house, we 'live' autism – it's a fundamental part of our family. I don't expect my extended family members to feel this level of understanding, but I do hope they will keep trying and being open to my children's unique needs and qualities. Sometimes acceptance and understanding can come from complete strangers. When we're out somewhere and someone else's child is becoming distressed or having a full-blown meltdown, I'll lock eyes with the other mom. It's a look that says: 'This is hard Mom, but you've got this.' It's a look that says: 'I know exactly how you feel, and it's okay.' It's such a comforting non-verbal exchange in that difficult moment. But it communicates an empathy that words never could.

Family members and friends, we need you. You can be the most supportive and helpful by asking questions. You can try to find out more about my child by spending more time with us. You can ask us what works best when you visit, or at a party or event. You can just sit in silence if we're having a tough time and you don't know what to say. Just be aware of how stigma can affect our children and how protective we feel of every bone in their body. And know that even when my child has perhaps physically hurt me, or had an hour-long meltdown, I still love them and feel just as protective of them and their needs. So tread carefully with language and just be open to finding out who our amazing children are.

KEY LEARNING POINTS FROM THIS CHAPTER:

- The words of family and friends can really impact the autistic child and their parents.
- The best-meaning comments in the world can feel like judgement.
- As a parent of an autistic child, it's likely you will spend a lot of your time explaining your child's needs and autism in general to other people.

- As a family member or friend of a child who is autistic, ask questions if you're unsure about something and know that the world looks and feels completely different for this child.
- Stigma effects autistic children and their families and results in increased stress and social exclusion.
- 'Parent blame' can further alienate and exclude families living with an autism diagnosis.
- Education and awareness can enhance understanding around autism and reduce stigma and prejudice.

Conclusion

Having an autistic child can be tough. The gruelling process of seeking a diagnosis and feeling like you're constantly questioning your own perceptions of your parenting is hard.

And adjusting to the actual diagnosis and the realisation that your child may need additional care and support across their lives can be emotionally very difficult. Coping with all of this, in addition to trying to meet your child's emotional and behavioural needs, combined with the judgement of your family and friends, can be too much sometimes. It can feel like everyone has an opinion and parents often feel judged for seeking or accepting a diagnosis of autism for their child. Family members and friends should be very mindful of their reactions to an autism diagnosis and do not say anything if you think you may say something which isn't helpful. Ask how you can help and if there's anything you can do to make the child feel more comfortable or included. Support your family member/friend with the decisions they make to help their child and just be open to how different their world is. Awareness campaigns and more open discussions about autism from early on (in school), can reduce the stigma experienced by many autistic children and their families.

6

CHALLENGING BEHAVIOUR

Introduction

I could write three books on this topic alone! But really, it sounds so manageable. A challenge is a task or a test to try to pass or achieve. In reality, challenging behaviour has the power to break a family, leave a child unable to attend school and can cause heartache for the child and those who love them. It's really important that you look at your child as separate to their behaviours. You can have a morning where they have perhaps done four really naughty or hurtful things. But they are still a little person who is feeling overwhelmed and need your help in some way to get through these events.

This chapter will discuss, honestly and openly, what challenging behaviour can feel like for a family. I will share my family's experiences with challenging behaviour and discuss what has helped me to help my children to behave in a kinder and safer way to both themselves and other people. What the experts say regarding challenging behaviour will be explored and some new ideas for responding to this will be considered.

My experiences

I walked in to the crèche to collect Ellie, she was six years old at the time and I was seven months pregnant. As I talked to the manager, Ellie wrapped her arms around my waist and hugged me. It was so lovely and not a very common occurrence where she would initiate a hug. Then I felt the searing pain on my bump. She had bitten me.

How do you react in that moment? In a room full of people, having experienced the severe sharp pain a bite causes, and with two big green eyes looking up at you, almost as a test to see if you would keep your cool? It was hard. Instinct told me to get as far away from this perceived threat which had inflicted such pain on me and so close to my unborn baby. But this 'threat' in fact came from my other baby whom I loved with all of my heart, yet felt an urge to run away from just in this moment. Ellie acted as though nothing had happened and I ushered her to the car where the tears fell. She didn't react, didn't shed tears and seeing other people sad didn't move her. She was sent to bed for 'time out' when we got home and we spoke about what happened and how wrong the behaviour was. But I knew this would have absolutely no impact whatsoever on Ellie, or her choice of future behaviour.

Daisy was much less subtle in her intent to hurt me, her dad or her brother Alex. I was lying in bed one Saturday morning with a broken toe. Daisy came into the room screaming that she wanted a treat 'now'. I said: 'No, it's not happening.' Then she punched me in my legs twice.

Alex was lying on the bathroom floor in school on one occasion, sobbing, rocking and repeating the same phrase over and over and over. The school called, because despite their best efforts this meltdown was just not stopping so we had to go in and collect him. My soul hurt thinking of this boy at twelve years old. What had happened to make him so upset? A very minor change in routine was the trigger. To most of the other children they likely didn't even notice this. But to Alex, this felt insurmountable. He was shaken and just could not cope with this change.

The games console has been a massive source of heartache in our house. Alex started displaying signs of addiction to this at around the age of eleven. This addiction meant that he had no other goal except to have access and would do whatever he had to, without thinking, in order to make this happen. I had been calling Alex to come and have dinner but he was totally engrossed in his game. After a while I said: 'That's it, I'm taking this games console away and you're having a break.' I bent down and started to unplug the wires and he lunged at me. Alex grabbed me by the back of my neck and wrestled me away from the console. I was scared. I hadn't realised just how big he had gotten and how he would be able to overpower me and so quickly at eleven years old. I found myself slowly retreating from the sitting room and just taking a moment to process what had happened. My son had manhandled me to prevent the games console being taken away.

The hardest part by far as a parent is anticipating and dreading a meltdown or any episode of challenging behaviour. It got to the point where a sound would make me jump and I felt anxious all of the time. I would be expecting something to happen particularly if we went anywhere like an event, so much so that I wouldn't enjoy it. And I've no doubt that my own anxiety and stress was felt by my children too on these days.

A 'tantrum' versus a 'meltdown'

In my experience, a tantrum is a short episode of screaming, shouting, refusing to follow requests and maybe hitting, throwing things or damaging property. A tantrum is usually displayed because of a specific need, want or issue. Consequently, a tantrum ordinarily subsides when the child has their demands met. So if they are screaming for extra TV time and you give in, the tantrum stops. Whereas a meltdown is not so logical. A meltdown has all the same characteristics of a tantrum: screaming, shouting, throwing things, hitting, etc. but is not eased by the meeting of your child's needs or demands. A meltdown can go on for hours and regardless of what you do to help your child, it may continue. Mr Alex in our house has the most challenging meltdowns. He will repeat the same phrase over and over and over, or will repeatedly open and bang doors.

A long time before his ASD diagnosis, we were flying to Portugal with our children when Alex had the most epic meltdown ever. It was so severe it was almost a made-for-TV meltdown and happened on the plane of all places. He kicked the seats in front of him, punched the seats behind him, screamed, rocked and repeated the same thing over and over and over again. My husband and I tried absolutely everything to negotiate with Alex, from bribes to alternatives and everything in between, to no avail. Being on a plane with everyone in such an enclosed space made it extra challenging. I could see the air hostesses whispering and all eyes were on us. As parents we felt immense pressure to make this behaviour stop. We repeatedly apologised to the passengers whose seats Alex was kicking and assured them this would stop. Eventually after about 25 minutes (which felt like a lifetime) Alex slowly but gradually came back down to his normal baseline behaviour. I felt the tears stinging my eyes but was conscious that I still had four children to look after and a plane full of eyes on our family. My husband squeezed my hand and said: 'It's okay love, he will be fine now.' Just before we landed the elderly lady who was sitting behind us came over. She said: 'You know you did such a wonderful job in that really difficult situation.' I began apologising profusely again. She said: 'No, you don't need to apologise, you did exactly what you needed to do and you're a good mom.' This is what I remember most about the whole trip.

Another momentous episode of challenging behaviour in our house happened when Ellie pushed Daniel down the stairs. Ellie was three years old and Daniel was two. We had a stairgate at the top of the stairs to keep the little people safe when playing upstairs. Ellie was like Houdini getting past any barriers we ever tried to fit such as press locks, window locks, car seats, etc. I was sweeping the kitchen downstairs when I heard the thumping and the dreaded bang. I still get goose bumps when I think of running to the bottom of the stairs. Daniel was lying in a foetal position on his head at the bottom of the stairs and was unconscious. I scooped him up and started screaming and shaking him, but he was limp in my arms. I ran out the front door and banged on my next door neighbours' doors with Daniel still in my arms. I screamed for help but no one was home. After what seemed like an eternity, Daniel slowly came back. He cried but was really drowsy. I sat on the floor inside my door and I cried and cried. But I was so relieved Daniel was awake. He then told me Ellie pushed him down the stairs. Ellie said she was sorry. I genuinely hadn't even considered this, I assumed Daniel had fallen. I can't remember who I called to look after Ellie while I brought Daniel to the hospital. He had a nasty bump on his head but seemed fine. We were there for a few hours for observation, and then went home.

One month later, we were back in the hospital again with Daniel for his second head injury within this time. I was in the room with them when Ellie pushed Daniel's highchair over with him in it and he banged his head off the fireplace. He didn't lose consciousness this time, but he had one of those giant egg-size lumps on his forehead. I was expecting some additional questions this time (two head injuries in four weeks) and perhaps a social work referral to check that all was okay in my home. But this didn't happen. I think that perhaps nowadays, it would have happened as we are more aware of child protection and the importance of this. I felt I was failing as a parent to protect my child from harm, even if it was from my other child. And then most notably, Daniel absolutely loved Ellie! He adored the ground she walked on and still does to this day. His tolerance and patience are endless and he has grown into the most gentle and kind young man.

This was an experience which made me question if I should be a parent at all. Why were other people's children not behaving like this? What was I doing wrong? And why did it feel like no professional I was interacting with at this time really got the gravity of how serious the behaviour was? I knew this was beyond acceptable or 'normal' behaviour (I hate that word).

How do you respond to challenging behaviour?

This really is the big question. And unfortunately there's no one, right answer. Even though I have lots of experience with challenging behaviour, it still causes ongoing struggles within our family. I've concluded that you might find a method that works for a while and you might then have to change it. What works for one of your autistic children, may not work for another. And with a meltdown, it may be more important to help to keep your child, other children and yourself safe during the meltdown rather than intervening to try to make the meltdown stop. Equally, creating a calm and predictable environment for your child can help prevent challenging behaviour from occurring in the first place. Some of the ideas in Chapter 9 discuss such methods in more detail.

I've tried absolutely every possible method of promoting positive behaviour you can think of. Some things didn't work at all, or some things worked for a while. But I always kept trying and still do. We have to as parents, keep trying, keep hopeful and keep working towards a calmer and happier family life and home. Some things that have worked and not worked for me with my younger children and challenging behaviour are discussed below.

Reward charts/star charts: you write a list of the behaviours you want to see more of e.g. talking calmly, sharing, being kind. Try to focus on the positives and goals for your child rather than 'no biting or hitting'. Reward charts are usually on public display in your house, so can be used as a source of pride for your child and a reason to praise them, rather than a list of bad behaviours or things that might make them feel embarrassed or ashamed. Give your child a star or sticker each time they show an effort in talking in a calm tone or in whatever goal you have agreed.

Achieving a whole day of calm behaviour can be very difficult for a child with autism and perhaps additional diagnoses. I have spilt the reward chart into morning, afternoon and evening sessions in an effort to give my child a chance to feel they are achieving something. I have even broken it down by hours rather than days when things are very challenging but I really want the child to have a chance to do their best and be praised for this. This isn't an overnight miracle which changes behaviour. But it does help initially at least. And if your child really struggles with managing and maintaining good behaviours, any opportunity to recognise and acknowledge them trying is a positive. Every moment where an incident of challenging behaviour or violent or aggressive behaviour doesn't happen is an example of positive behaviour. So do acknowledge this and make it a habit to tell your child how amazing they are and how much you love them at every opportunity. It's important that our children know how much we love them, even if they are behaving violently or aggressively. We love them even on the hardest of days, or even when they hurt us. We may think they know this, but they might not. So do tell them this, always.

Time out: this was a disaster in my house! Daisy hits Alex, then I sit Daisy on the bottom step of the stairs for a planned two minutes. I explain to Daisy: 'You are here because you hit Alex and that's not nice. You need to sit on the step for two minutes and think about what you did.' Twenty minutes later after the 796th time Daisy got up off the step I would usually give up. This just didn't work for us for any of our children. But it is still worth a try for you. It's a good method if it works as it's a short, swift response to bad behaviour, and when the time on the step is complete, that's it you move on to a fresh start. It communicates to your child that the behaviour is unacceptable, or that there's a better way to behave. For example, if your child hurts you or another child intentionally, time out can present time for them to reflect on their choice of behaviour and give the injured party a chance to breathe and recover. If you have more than one child, and if it works, time out can give you the space to comfort your other child if they have been hurt. However, the time out spot should not be outside and shouldn't cause your child severe distress. If they are frightened or scared by time out then this is not an appropriate method of trying to promote more positive behaviours. It should feel like a quiet time, rather than a time which upsets your child. It's a pause or a break to reflect, and shouldn't cause your child major upset. Remember that autism and any other condition your child is diagnosed with can make challenging behaviour much more frequent or common. Therefore, methods like time out that parents of neurotypical children might use regularly might not be appropriate if the frequency of challenging behaviour is ten times a day. So weigh up the benefits and challenges of each response to this behaviour based on what your child needs, what you need and what will benefit your family most at that time. There really is no one-size-fits-all with autism. And what works for a neurotypical child often doesn't work for an autistic child as the frequency and severity of the challenging behaviour is completely different.

Fresh starts: these are massively important when your child has any condition or difficulty which may make it more challenging for them to control their behaviour. They involve being able to start again, afresh and without being reminded of their bad behaviour from earlier in that day or week. If your child has a clean slate, it's probably more achievable for them to maintain this and stay in the green. But if your child is being reprimanded an hour after an incident then they may start to view themselves as bad or naughty and may feel there's no point in trying to behave in a more positive way. For example: if Alex throws a toy at Daisy on Friday, and the first thing I say on Saturday morning is: 'I can't believe you threw that toy', or 'I'm so upset with this behaviour', etc. Alex could feel like there's no point in trying to behave differently on this occasion.

You need to find what works for you and your child. But first and foremost you need to model the behaviours you want to child to display. If you shout then your child will view this as acceptable behaviour. If you stay calm, and are consistent, these are the behaviours your child will model. Equally, if Daisy is screaming because her clothes are really irritating her, or if Alex bangs a door because he feels overwhelmed, I don't respond to these episodes as 'bad behaviour'. I try to relieve the distress they are feeling and we move on. I will speak really calmly and in an even tone, and try to be calming and supportive in order to help them feel better. This really works. So what another parent might consider to be 'bad behaviour' or 'intentionally disruptive behaviour', parents of autistic children may not. Do what you feel is right for your child. And trial and error is often the most effective way of finding what works best.

Most times when my children misbehaved, it was in an effort to communicate something they were unable to say verbally. Children with high-functioning autism may be verbal, but still have substantial challenges in communicating. Daisy would scream the house down and be very defiant if she had a throat infection, which happened regularly. Alex refusing to get dressed for school has been a way of letting me know he is struggling with a change that happened in class. While Ellie has become so overwhelmed with anxiety in the run-up to an event like a school tour, that she would kick me and hit her siblings. I've learned that when my child is violent, defiant, oppositional or generally going out of their way to be difficult, they are more often than not trying to tell me something. Knowing this doesn't make coping with the behaviour any easier though, nor does it always help to reduce or stop the behaviour. Most often we, as parents, are firefighting and trying to get through this hour, or this day, whilst keeping our children and ourselves safe. This is the reality for many families with an autistic child/children and something we rarely discuss openly. Some days are so challenging and difficult that making it to the end of the day without anyone getting seriously hurt or physically harmed can feel like an achievement. Having other children to protect and protecting your autistic child from themselves can be a permanent worry.

So with all this insight I have … and all of this experience … surely we no longer have any episodes of challenging behaviours in our house? We sure do, and possibly always will. But I can definitely cope better now and try to keep everyone safe. I also have more tools in my toolkit for exploring the behaviour and what might be causing this. But it still sometimes feels out of control. There are still days I'm praying for bedtime and that I just need to have a good cry. However, my self-care routine (discussed in chapter 11) has literally saved me on tough days. And having a strong support network in my immediate family and close friends has also been a godsend. And professionals have and will hopefully continue to support my family in navigating this autism journey and the behaviours which come with it.

What do the experts say?

Chiang suggests that autistic children have communication difficulties and may use challenging behaviour in their attempts to communicate.[72] Even children with good verbal ability struggle with verbalising their needs effectively. Bedrossian[73] argues that meltdowns can be your child's response when they:

- Experience sensory overload
- Have too many tasks to complete
- Have experienced an unexpected change or
- Feel they can't succeed or accomplish what is expected of them

Mazefsky[74] describes meltdowns as explosions of anger which can escalate into violent and potentially dangerous events. Challenging behaviour can stem from what is happening around the child and their difficulty in coping with this.[75] This is partly explained by systems theory which proposes that the child both affects and is affected by everything in their lives such as school, their home environment, their family life, and so on.[76] I've always found this theory helpful as it can help parents understand when our child is displaying challenging behaviour, and can also shed light on how this can impact us as parents. Then the cycle continues with each of us interacting with and affecting one another. For example, if Alex is having a hard morning before school and screaming or refusing to get dressed. This affects me as I'm getting stressed, so my responses to Alex are stressed, and he feels even more overwhelmed, and the challenging behaviour increases. I'm also then less patient with Daisy and the morning is then in danger of becoming a giant disaster! If instead I can choose how I react and if I react super-calmly and without stress, the situation can diffuse a lot more quickly. Alex's distress reduces, my stress reduces and we can usually get on with our morning and get out the door.

Parental stress is substantially higher in parents of autistic children compared to other conditions, largely due to challenging behaviour.[77] Lots of things can impact our ability to parent an autistic child and to respond to their needs in the way we need to. Parents who themselves have had a difficult childhood and experienced poor parenting may find responding to their child effectively even more difficult.[78] Montaque and colleagues in 2018 in their research found that many parents of autistic children live with a sense of fear and dread concerning when the next meltdown will occur.[78]

Moyes proposes that planning is essential for parents in responding to challenging behaviour.[79] Rather than waiting for the behaviour to occur, having a plan in place to reduce the likelihood of the behaviour occurring in the first place can help parents to feel empowered. One suggestion Moyes makes is providing an 'escape plan'. Often used in the classroom, this is useful if you know your child has had difficulty with a situation or place in the past. It gives them the option to leave or exit in advance and can reduce their anxiety levels and potentially reduce challenging behaviours.[79] For example, giving your child a card to show if they're feeling overwhelmed or need a break, or giving them a signal they can use to tell you they need to stop what they're doing. It might be to touch their nose, or clap their hands. This could work during tasks they find stressful like brushing teeth, doing homework or when they are in close proximity to other people.

Lewis suggests that using rewards can be really helpful for encouraging more positive behaviours.[80] Identifying the behaviours you want to see more of, rather than the behaviours you want to stop, is the best way to help your child to succeed. For example with Ellie we created our own home-made reward chart. We sat together at the table and decided on the behaviours we wanted to see more of: 'Be kind to Daniel, talk in a nice calm voice,' etc. I gave Ellie glitter and colours to decorate the chart so she could really take ownership. The rewards we had were cinema trips, extra TV time or a sweet treat. We put this on the fridge so we wouldn't forget about it and so Ellie could get lots of praise for doing so well. Lewis also recommends rotating and updating rewards to help keep your child motivated and interested!

More recent literature suggests presents contrasting views on whether time outs are an appropriate response to responding to challenging behaviours. Yet considerable research proposes that time out, when used alongside rewards and praise, can be effective in reducing problematic behaviours, as reported by Morawska and Sanders in 2011.[81] Research as recent as 2017, by Corralejo, Jensen and Greathouse,[82] found that when undertaken for very short periods of time, time out reduces sibling aggression. This review of multiple studies found that shorter periods of time for time out were actually more effective in promoting positive behaviour.

The evolution of the terms used to describe giving a child space and time to think when they are feeling overwhelmed is important as we become more aware based on continued research concerning what works. Lantieri (2008)[83] introduced the idea of the peace corner within educational settings. This space provides the child with an opportunity for reflection in a safe space and perhaps a space with comforting items like fidget toys or calming visuals. Such ideas promote the idea of supporting rather than punishing problematic behaviours and providing space for the restoration of calming feelings and behaviour. According to Housman (2017),[84] a peace corner promotes the child's mental health and wellbeing, while encouraging the child to build their ability to regulate their emotions, with adult support.

Coogan discusses nonviolent resistance (NVR) in his book about responding to child-to-parent violence.[85] The key focus of non-violent resistance is about creating and maintaining more positive relationships between parents and their children. Schorr-Sapir and colleagues found through their study that NVR reduces parental distress and improves behaviours and emotional well-being for children.[86]

Non-violent resistance focuses on the here and now (rather than what might happen or has happened), and is based on the parental response to challenging and violent behaviours.[85] According to Coogan, non-violent resistance isn't a definitive solution with a success rate of 100%, but it is a tool parents can use to guide them in responding to child-to-parent violence.[85] The key principles of non-violent resistance are:

- Creating consistency and reassurance for the child in the parental response to their behaviour
- Preventing escalation when aggressive or violent behaviour occurs
- Empowering parents to develop skills to reduce violence in the home
- Engaging 'supporters' to act as positive reinforcements for parents.[86]

The idea of NVR proposes that parents model the calm and responsive behaviours they would like their child to display. So how does it work in practice?

- Explain to your child what NVR is and that you are introducing this to respond to aggressive or violent behaviours.
- Resist engagement with their child which could escalate or aggravate the situation.[87] You might feel like shouting if they are shouting, but completely avoiding any aggressive behaviour is key.
- Increase your presence in your child's life as a parent. Aim to spend more time with them, be at home more, or to really engage with them when you are together.
- Don't give in to the aggressive behaviour, as this communicates to the child that this type of behaviour will work to get their way.
- Reassure your child that you love them and you will love them no matter what. Even if they are screaming at you or trying to

hurt you, keep reassuring them that you're there and you love them.

- Speak to your child after the aggressive behaviour about what happened and that this is not acceptable. Ask what their thoughts are on how to prevent this type of incident from occurring again. Stay with your child, allow silence and reassure them that you love them and are committed to NVR.
- Share with your supporter everything that's happening. Let them know what you're doing, how it's progressing and how you're feeling. If needed or preferred, your supporter can speak to your child about what's happening and support you with your commitment to NVR.[88]

Supporters are family members or close friends of parents who are acting in a supportive capacity and will offer consistent encouragement and reassurances to parents.[87] They will act as a sounding board, a confidant and a source of support for the parent as they introduce and maintain NVR within their families. This supporter role is vital and requires a commitment to stay with the parent throughout the process, in order to be most effective.

A really helpful parent guide on NVR, called 'Non-violent Resistance (NVR): Guidelines for parents of children or adolescents with violent or destructive behaviours', can be found at oxleas.nhs.uk, by clicking into the Advice section, and from there to: Children and Young People's Services > Non-Violent Resistance (NVR) > Parent booklets.

KEY LEARNING POINTS FROM THIS CHAPTER:

- Challenging behaviour is very difficult and stressful for both parents and autistic children.
- Challenging behaviour can create an anxious and fearful home environment.
- Challenging behaviour is usually your child's way of trying to communicate something.
- Trying different methods of responding to challenging behaviour to see what works best for your child is important.

- Your reaction to violent or aggressive behaviour is key to deescalating the situation and restoring calm.
- NVR is a useful parenting technique which can help you to support your child in reducing aggressive and violent behaviours.

Conclusion

This chapter has explored the challenge that is challenging behaviour for autistic children and their families. Challenging behaviour could be screaming, shouting, throwing objects, biting, pushing or hitting another person, or threatening to harm someone else. Autistic children might display challenging behaviour when they feel uncomfortable, overwhelmed, threatened or are coping with a change they hadn't expected. Parents of autistic children may worry about when an episode of challenging behaviour might occur, and worry that they won't be able to cope with this. Aggressive and violent behaviour is not okay and should not be accepted as a normal part of autism. Parents should be supported and empowered to respond to challenging behaviour in a way which will reduce further aggression and restore calm in their home. Techniques such as planning for challenging behaviour, remaining calm in your responses and using rewards were discussed. Non-violent resistance (NVR) has been identified as a really useful tool for parents to help their child to reduce violent behaviours.

7

FRIENDS OR NO FRIENDS

We walked into the soft play area, Ellie (then aged seven), Daniel and I. It was 4.00 p.m. on a school day. I paid and the kids took off their shoes and began heading towards the bouncy castle. I spotted one of Ellie's school friends from her class. Then I saw another, and another. I felt my cheeks flush ... I could tell people were watching me. I looked around and saw four of the other school moms from Ellie's class. They looked surprised ... it slowly dawned on me what had happened – we had just walked into a birthday party for another little girl in Ellie's class ... which she hadn't been invited to. A little girl awkwardly came over and said: 'Ellie ... I wasn't expecting you.' My eyes filled as I gathered up my kids and held my tears until we reached the car. Ellie kept asking what was wrong – it was a blessing she didn't know. Now she doesn't remember this incident at all, but I'll never forget.

Introduction

By far the most challenging part of my journey without question, has been the issue of friends, or lack thereof. To see your child feeling the hurt and rejection of other children not wanting to play with them is absolutely heart-breaking. This chapter will discuss the idea of friendships and supporting your child socially. My own experiences will highlight the variation in the social ability and preferences of autistic children, and how you as a parent can help your child to develop and maintain friendships. Helping your child to cope with rejection and exclusion will be explored, and the practical ways you can encourage friendships for your child will be discussed. An overview of what the experts say regarding autism and friendships will be provided. This chapter will highlight the social challenges many autistic children have. We know our children may struggle to communicate or not notice social cues, but what can we do help them to develop socially and make friends?

My experiences

Ellie had always wanted friends, but always struggled to keep friends. Watching your child trying so hard to be liked and feel wanted and feeling unable to change things for them is soul destroying. Not getting invited to birthday parties, not being included in the games at lunchtime or never being invited for playdates are common experiences for many autistic children. And in my experience, this is more a problem identified and experienced by girls as opposed to boys. One of my daughters has felt rejection and exclusion throughout her life as she tried to fit in. She has ended up in fist fights, online altercations and screaming matches on the street. Whereas my other daughter finds things much easier and masks so well that she fits in and has lots of friends. So as parents we need to follow their lead and support our autistic kids as much as we need to, to build and maintain friendships and relationships.

Alex has always had lots of friends. His bluntness (so far at least) tends to draw other children. And I've found with all three of my autistic children that children with additional needs tend to find each other. This is such a wonderful thing to see. Alex tends to ignore people when they say hello, and tends to shout at inappropriate times (like when things are quiet). Alex's stims are rocking, hand flapping and pacing back and forth. Yet other boys want to be near him and it's such a wonderful thing to see. And such a different experience from when Ellie was this age. Boys appear less concerned with being liked, or included, and this tends to make them less self-conscious.

We walked very nervously into the open evening for Alex's new secondary school. No children from his primary school were going to the same secondary school. One boy was waving at Alex from across the room. Alex waved back then looked at the floor. I asked who this boy was, but Alex said 'I don't know'. We all had to do a scavenger hunt as part of the ice breakers for the open evening and two more boys came over and said hi to Alex. They asked him about Minecraft and talked about other boys they knew. Alex didn't really respond. But they didn't seem to mind. These two boys came back with another boy who said: 'Hey, Alex!' Alex sarcastically replied that everyone didn't have to follow him to his new school.

Later I found out that two of these boys were Alex's friends from Scouts, while two more were from the basketball club Alex goes to for kids with dyspraxia. Alex never talked about his friends but I knew he was happy in his activities. Sometimes he didn't want to go. But now in hindsight, every time I persevered and really encouraged and persuaded him to go, it was completely worth the effort.

Some autistic children will be aware that they have few friends or social opportunities. But other children may have greater needs and may not be aware at all if they are being excluded or have no friends.

One day I was standing for 30 minutes with the other parents at the school gate waiting for Ellie to come back from her school tour. I was hopeful it was a good day for her as the school hadn't called to report any incident (phone calls during the school day are rarely good news!). The bus pulled up and all the children came off chatting, shouting, laughing excitedly. I scanned the children for Ellie but I couldn't see her. She was one of the last to get off the bus and I knew as soon as I saw her little face that she had had a tough day. She ran to me and burst in to big sad sobs as I hugged her. She had sat on her own on the bus ... both ways. No one sat with her. And she didn't have the confidence to ask anyone to sit with her. She was alone for most of the day.

We tried super hard to help Ellie to make and maintain friendships. From giant birthday parties with a nail and make-up artist coming to our house to do all the girls nails, to lunches out with friends in local restaurants, sleepovers, every activity or club you could imagine, and lots of play dates. I think in hindsight I projected this need on to Ellie.

Interestingly Ellie said the most profound thing to me about two years ago when she was 17. I was asking her if she had plans for the weekend and I suggested she message one of the girls from school and meet up with them. Her response blew me away. She said: 'Mam, I don't have an issue with not having friends, it doesn't bother me a bit, I'm happy. This is your issue.' And she was completely right. My feelings of hurt and rejection for her from her younger experiences, combined with my need for friendship and connection, made *me* feel that Ellie needed friends. But these are my issues, not hers. Ellie is a very confident, beautiful and resilient young woman who still doesn't have this need that I have for lots of friends. She goes out, meets people when she wants to, and has a partner. She is happy. She doesn't care what anyone thinks of her, doesn't do things to please people or make them like her. She couldn't care less and it's quite liberating to see. Part of me envies her carefree approach. Ellie is now in a position to offer advice to me on how to help her younger siblings with social opportunities and friendships. She has the experience of her nineteen years to share, and of having me as a parent. She is direct with me in telling me about mistakes I made and what she thinks I should do or not do in order to help her siblings. I am really grateful to have this insight and guidance from her.

How can you help your child to make friends?

Our children may need additional help and support to build and maintain friendships. You may find yourself arranging playdates for your teenager or hosting, even when it's someone else's turn. And that's completely okay. I've found that networking with the parents of children your child likes can be a great way of encouraging your child's friendships. Other autism moms are amazing, and their children aren't at all phased by stims and completely accept your child exactly how they are. I have a strong network of autism moms, many of whom I've met through my children. We take turns hosting playdates and also share the driving when it comes to getting to and from activities. This helps on a day where Alex may feel like skipping basketball. But knowing his friend will be picking him up has been a great motivator. Cousins are also a wonderful source of friendship for children with additional needs. Their familiarity with your child means they won't be horrified if a meltdown happens and may be more accepting of difficulties your child may have with turn taking or controlling their emotions. Any opportunity for interaction should be encouraged.

Clubs and groups are often a traumatic and anxiety-filled experience for our children. It can take weeks of preparation and planning to even attend for the first time. Your child will beg you not to send them, will plead to skip it for just this week. Yet I can safely say now that joining clubs has been a very positive experience for each of my autistic children. When Ellie was small, I caved after a few weeks of dragging her kicking and screaming to Irish dancing or drama and didn't make her go back. Also, a few episodes of challenging behaviour or the fear that this might happen at a club is another real concern. But with Alex and Daisy their needs were just different. And maybe being older and having some life experience made me approach things differently. Also, now that Ellie is an adult I can ask for advice about these things. She's an amazing resource for me in my parenting. For example, I asked Ellie if she wished I had persisted a bit more with her attending clubs and she said yes, she would like to have stayed with an activity. To have an autistic voice to give me such guidance and insight, and an autistic voice of a daughter who knows me and my parenting inside out, is amazing!

So rather than folding and the kids dropping out of an activity, I try to find a compromise. We can take a week off. We can maybe attend for half an hour instead of an hour, or we use good old-fashioned rewards (bribes) of McDonalds to sweeten the deal. You will know after a couple of months if your child is benefitting from attending and you can make a decision then about continuing or not. Daisy, after doing Scouts on Zoom for the last seven months, finally said the Scouts' prayer last night out loud. For all that time she never said it (they say it together as a group), she just sat there. But this was okay. Because now she has done it and all parents of ASD children will know that this was a massive achievement! We were so proud of her and can see how much she is developing in confidence and socially from attending. If something gets too much? We skip it. If there's an outing that causes anxiety or an activity that makes them feel scared, we discuss it. We talk about all the things that could happen, how they are feeling and how I can help them to feel less worried. If this doesn't help, we just say we're going to sit this one out. And it has always been perfectly okay with all the leaders of the groups my children attend. Also, for your child to know you're listening and trying to help them is reassuring in itself and usually helps them to feel less worried or stressed. These clubs (Scouts, basketball and swimming lessons) have helped Alex and Daisy to make lots of friends, helped them to get more comfortable in unfamiliar situations and give them the opportunity to build upon their social skills.

Coaching your child when they are interacting with other children can be helpful, for example: your child might need prompting to reply if they are asked a question; reminding your child about taking turns or sharing can be helpful; or prompting your child to play more gently if they are playing rough. Being near your child when they are making friends is also important to keep both them and the other child safe. You may need to intervene if your child is becoming upset or aggressive. Even still, it is possible your child may lash out or hurt the other child. But if you are near you can intervene quickly and diffuse the situation. I've found children forget quickly after an outburst and are friends again within minutes. However, other parents aren't always this forgiving. They want to protect their child and this is completely understandable. Therefore, building relationships with one or two other parents can be a great way to smooth over minor incidents and get back on track with friendships. Cousins in particular have been the best friend my children could ask for. They are their first friends and just accept them exactly as they are which is so lovely.

Social skills groups are a great way for autistic children to learn how to feel more comfortable socially. These are usually offered by the organisation where your child received their diagnosis, and usually consist of a small number of children. Social skills clubs look at feelings, how children express these, facial expressions and improving confidence. Your child's resource teacher or special needs assistant can also support your child in small groups in school to build upon their new skills.

Structuring social opportunities/playdates can help your child to feel less worried about this and they will know exactly what to expect. Anxiety can happen when children are unsure of what to expect or if there's uncertainty. So charts can be a good way to communicate exactly what will happen. For example:

- ☐   10.00 a.m.   We will collect your friend
- ☐   10.30 a.m.   We will go to the park
- ☐   12.00 p.m.   We will come home and have lunch
- ☐   1.00 p.m.   We will play board games
- ☐   2.00 p.m.   We will drop your friend home

Many autistic children like to spend time alone. Supporting your child to do this is important too. School and social activities are exhausting for our children, so letting them know that they can watch TV alone, or spend time in their bedroom, will help them to cope. Having time alone allows our children to take a complete break from the effort of communicating and interacting, and to recharge their batteries. Weighted blankets, dim lighting or a bean bag can also help with this winding-down process. We tend to worry about children being alone in their rooms. But I find this is a necessary breather for my children and something they really need in order to cope when they feel socially exhausted or overwhelmed.

Looking for alternative ways of communicating and maintaining friendships might be helpful for your child. Lockdown presented these opportunities for my children. Attending clubs on Zoom, having Facetime with school friends and, for the first time ever, writing letters, was a great lesson for us all. If seeing other children face to face is too much sometimes, a Zoom date could be ideal. You could arrange a short Zoom with one of their friends to catch up on their news. You staying with them is also important as you can help prompt if things are quiet or if your child is struggling to interact.

Summer camps are a really important way for your child to maintain and build upon their social skills over the summer months. Eight weeks is a very long time for your child to be at home and maybe not interacting with other children very much. A part-time, drop-in, or once-off summer camp is a great way for your child to socialise and make new friends. There are some autism-specific summer camps, and some mainstream summer camps may also be appropriate for autistic children.

Modelling behaviours such as turn-taking in conversations, telling jokes and maybe understanding things like sarcasm can also be helpful for your child. Neurotypical people instinctively know how to do these things. But often autistic children don't. By explaining things as they happen, our children are constantly learning. For example, if your child tells a joke and it's funny laughing and telling them this is a funny joke is communicating clearly and teaching them about feedback. Equally, if your child tells twenty jokes one after another and they don't make sense, or become annoying, telling your child this (gently) is also helpful. This will help them to understand how other people may receive their communication attempts.

What do the experts say?

Friendships and social opportunities can improve mental health and even academic achievement in autistic children.[89] Most autistic children do want to make friends and have social opportunities.[89] Research acknowledges however, that autistic children have difficulty in recognising and responding to language, emotional needs of other people and social cues.[90] Bauminger and colleagues report that some autistic children interact better with one other child, as opposed to a group.[91] This study in Israel also concluded that many autistic children are not fully aware of their interactional abilities. Our children may misinterpret the effectiveness of their communication and closeness with their peers.[91] I've experienced this with one of my children and it was heart-breaking. They may not 'get' if another child is rejecting them and does not reciprocate the friendship.

Both parents and teachers have a much more significant role in promoting friendships for autistic children compared to neurotypical children. Examples of how teachers can help autistic children to develop friendships include directing children to pair together for activities or work in small groups.[92] Chang and colleagues in their research found that autistic children who have friendships in school have better communication and attention skills as a result.[92] Although, within this study and consistent with previous studies, just 20% of autistic children surveyed had a friendship in school.[92][93]

Bauminger and Kasari[94] report that some children with high-functioning autism may misinterpret reciprocal friendships. This is certainly something I have experienced with my own children. Daisy may call Molly her bestie and view her as her most favourite friend. Yet in reality Daisy and Molly may have very little interaction and Daisy may not notice when Molly is disinterested or does not want to play with her. This is very hard to watch. When we see our little people really trying, and not understanding the feedback they are getting from other children. But equally, I do wonder if this is a blessing in a way? They are unaware so are not recognising potential rejection, or coping with the negative feelings which come with this.

One study in 2020 found that as autistic children get older, they worry that the stigma around having a diagnosis of autism can be a barrier to forming friendships.[95] Some young people interviewed in their study reported people treating them differently when they found out they were autistic and that they had a more negative view of themselves due to their diagnosis.[95] This internalised stigma can prevent autistic children from seeking and maintaining friendships. Cridland and their colleagues suggest that autistic girls struggle more in adolescence with social interaction compared to autistic boys.[96] They suggest that the complex nature of female relationships can present additional challenges for autistic girls as they need to engage more on an emotional level.[96] Stigma surrounding autism is something which is still very evident within society. Today Ellie often doesn't tell people she's autistic as she worries about how she will be judged.

Key learning points from this chapter:

- Try lots of different activities and see what your child is interested in and where they feel most comfortable. Scouts focus on multiple skills, activities and strengths. So this has been a good fit for my children.
- Put yourself out there socially and make the connections with other parents that your child may not be able to make for themselves just yet.

- Nurture the friendships your child has. Host the playdates, do Zoom calls or even help your child to write a letter to post to their friend. Every single interaction for our children is a learning experience.
- Enrol your child in social skills groups or independent living skills groups. They won't want to go (in my experience), but will be glad they went! Do as much of this as possible before the teenage years when they will say no and you won't be able to persuade them!
- Adults have a greater role in supporting autistic children to interact and develop their social skills.
- Stigma can impact social opportunities for autistic children.

Conclusion

This chapter introduced the issue of friendship for children living with a diagnosis of autism (or indeed while they are awaiting assessment). Seeing your child alone and without friends is undoubtedly one of the hardest parts of autism parenting. You just want to protect them from this hurt and make everything okay. Feeling rejected and excluded by their peers can and does create substantial distress for children who are different. There are things you can do as a parent, as identified within this chapter, to support your child with friendships. In my experience joining clubs and connecting with other moms are the most effective methods. The research also highlights the need for parents and teachers to support autistic children in building relationships with other children.

8

MEDICATION

Introduction

Medication for autistic children is something that most parents struggle with making a decision about. Should we medicate our children? Is it right to medicate your child? And will medication make them 'not them' anymore? The moral and ethical dilemmas that arise at even the mention of medication for autistic children present substantial challenges for most parents.

This chapter will discuss medication as a response to some of the difficulties autism presents to a child. The aim of this chapter is to give you more information regarding medication and how this may impact your child and family. Our own experiences with medication will be shared and the ethical dilemmas parents face in deciding whether or not to medicate their child will be explored. The views of professionals concerning medication for autistic children will also be considered. However, in this chapter I will not identify the brand or type of medication used, as I would not want to influence in any way your decision to trial a medication. Equally, the research articles and professionals I refer to within this chapter are also based on my interpretation and shouldn't replace your own research and speaking in depth with your child's service provider. This chapter will present you with an overview of things most of us think and worry about when considering medication for our child, and will hopefully help you to feel more informed about this and perhaps less anxious about the 'what-ifs'.

My experiences

The number of my family members and close friends who said: 'But you're not going to medicate her?' Or: 'She will be like a zombie if you give her medicine.' Or even: 'I think that's just really wrong to medicate a child.' Each time someone said something like this it chipped away at my self-worth and my perceived ability as a parent. Because I couldn't wait for my child to start medication. We were desperate ... beyond desperate for Ellie to be okay, for our family life to return to some kind of normal. I felt like screaming: 'Do you know how many other things we've tried? Do you realise how much this is a last resort for us?' It was horrific to feel the judgement of other people and so openly, on an issue which could potentially change Ellie's life for the better and make our family life a more stable and happy one.

First and foremost, medication is not used to treat autism. Medication can be used to treat some of the challenges autistic children face as a result of their autism, or another condition that they have. Ellie is also diagnosed with ADHD and ODD. The main concern for us as parents was always Ellie's ability to control her impulses and not physically hurt other people. So we tried many different therapies and supports to help Ellie to better cope with her emotions and her responses to stressful situations. However, as a last resort, we eventually considered medication.

Guilt is a really common feeling parents have when they are considering medication for their child. But this was one feeling I didn't have. We had tried so many other options for four years prior to considering medication. I knew we had exhausted every other viable option and that medication truly and honestly was a very last resort for us.

So what did we try first? We tried every imaginable type of therapy and intervention you could think of, some of which are listed here:

• *Homeopathy*: we visited a homeopath for an appointment and she did an assessment of Ellie's needs and then gave us some herbal tablets. These worked well for about a week. I was hopeful. But then they stopped working. We tried a different blend of herbal remedies but these didn't work.

- *Family therapy*: this definitely helped. It helped us to identify what works and how we could cope better when things were super tough.
- *Play therapy*: uses play to communicate with children and better understand them. This was an amazing resource to be offered at this time as play therapy was not readily available when Ellie was small (and is very difficult to source now). Play therapy didn't make any major impact on Ellie's behaviour, but it was insightful in that the play therapist identified early on that there was more to Ellie's needs than ADHD and ODD. She spotted the very subtle signs of autism which girls who are masking display.
- *Parenting course*: I discussed this in another chapter. I learned things that could help me in my parenting, but parenting courses are not an appropriate response to a child with ADHD or autism. They can be a helpful add-on, but the suggestion that my child's needs were due to my parenting capacity or approach was quite hurtful.
- *Social skills groups*: these helped Ellie to develop her abilities socially. They didn't really have any impact long-term, but it was a place Ellie didn't feel like the 'bold child' for once.
- *Biofeedback training*: this is a brain training non-invasive intervention for children with impulse control issues, ADHD and challenging behaviour. They wear a hat with sensors to monitor their brain activity, while they play a computer game with their mind. It sounds bizarre but the idea is that when the child uses a calming positive part of their brain, the game progresses for them (the spaceship moves, or they can go left or right). But if their brain is frustrated or angry, the spaceship won't move. This was the most expensive alternative therapy we tried and cost approximately €1,500 for a set of sessions. This had zero effect on promoting positive behaviour.
- *Dietician*: Ellie met with a dietician who checked what foods she was intolerant to. The result was all processed foods. She advised that we don't give Ellie any processed foods or anything

from a packet. This was not at all helpful and although we did trial this advice for a short period of time, it was too difficult for our family to implement around modern established eating habits. And unfortunately made no difference to the frequency of hyperactivity, impulsiveness or challenging behaviour.

Additional note on two alternative therapies we tried with Daisy and mostly to help sleep and calming behaviour:

- *Craniosacral therapy*: This is a hands over non-invasive therapy aimed at 'enhancing the body's natural capacity for healing'.[97] This was a lovely calming experience, but unfortunately didn't make a difference with sleep or behaviour in our case.
- *Bioenergy therapy*: again, this is a hands over and sometimes hands-on therapy, which attempts to rebalance or align the body's energy which vibrates at different levels.[98] Bioenergy healing helps the body to recover from blockages of energy which can cause pain, insomnia or discomfort. Daisy was two when we tried about six sessions of bioenergy healing. The experience was a calm and relaxing one and, unbelievably, Daisy slept for her first full night (ever) after her first session! Unfortunately, this didn't happen again, but even that one night was a very welcome break from sleeplessness.

Sometimes due to the severity of your child's needs, medication might actually be the first port of call and this is absolutely okay too. Child psychiatrists who prescribe these medications don't do so lightly. In my experience they don't medicate children at the drop of a hat. It has to be necessary and the risks weighed carefully against the benefits. Your child's doctor will monitor them closely when they start meds and ensure that these meds are the right ones for your child. Do note though that often blood tests are required prior to and during trials of medications. So this presents a whole other set of challenges. Blood tests aren't nice for any child. But for an autistic child getting bloods taken can be a different story altogether. Discuss your concern with your child's doctor. We've met some truly talented medical professionals who make the process of blood tests the least traumatic it can be for your child.

Ellie ran out of our GP's surgery one day when she was getting a vaccination. She was absolutely terrified. Daniel had just got his (I think it was the swine flu jab) and he was only a toddler. When Ellie saw him and knew she was next she became so panicked that she left the doctor's office screaming, ran past the waiting room, out of the surgery and onto the road. I had to leave Daniel with the GP while I chased after her. She was so, so scared, absolutely terrified. Everyone was staring at us and there some not-so-nice looks from people in the waiting room, which didn't help. I promised her she didn't have to get the jab but I needed her to come back in with me to get Daniel. It took a while to convince her and eventually we went back in, me reassuring her all the way. And did I make her get the jab in the end? No way. She was so frightened … way more than a fear of needles, this was complete panic. I promised her she wouldn't have to get it and that things were going to be okay and I kept my promise. Keeping promises and communicating to your kids that they can trust you is key. It's got me out of more binds than I can count over the years. If your child trusts you and you reassure them or promise them something when they are very distressed, they will believe you and this will reassure them when they feel overwhelmed or panicked.

*Note: Do I ever tell white lies to my children? Absolutely. Daisy thinks we have air conditioning in our house for about three years now. When she's too hot she now asks us to put on the cold air … so we tell her we do!

Eventually, when we were offered medication for Ellie, we were desperate. Desperate to help her and desperate for her to have a day in school or at home where she wasn't causing chaos, hurting other children or getting into trouble. We were desperate for her to feel comfortable in school, to feel accepted and to feel liked (rather than constantly viewed as naughty by her peers and excluded and rejected socially as a result).

So we started the first medication and initially didn't notice much of a difference. About a week in we noticed Ellie was a bit more tired, but definitely calmer. We saw a reduction in violent outbursts so felt that the meds were starting to work. Side effects are very tough when they happen, and this is when the guilt really did kick in for me. Ellie started feeling unwell about two weeks into her first trial of medication. She said she could feel her heart pounding in her chest. I felt with my hand and I could feel it too. This medication was discontinued after the second time Ellie experienced this fast-pounding heartbeat.

The second medication we tried really did slow Ellie down. I was so torn, as behaviourally she was doing so much better. And for the first time in many years we were functioning like a typical family. The teacher did notice that Ellie was sleepy in class, so the dose was tweaked when we checked in with Ellie's doctor. However, I started to notice that Ellie was losing weight. She was quite slim already, and within the normal height and weight range for her age. However, about six weeks in, her weight loss was about four pounds, which was fairly substantial for an eight year old, so we stopped using this medication immediately. I do remember feeling very supported by Ellie's medical team and felt reassured that they were checking how she was doing, while trialling meds very regularly. At this point as we had tried two of the most common and most effective medications and both had caused harmful side effects, so doctors advised that Ellie should not try another medication at this point.

So for the next four or five years, Ellie didn't take any medication. But as her teenage years crept in ... my God, did things become more challenging. Meltdowns were more extreme and my ability to manage Ellie physically as she got bigger decreased. I remember being terrified when she banged a door and I couldn't physically stop her from hitting or pushing me. Things became unmanageable when Ellie was about fourteen and we were still attending medical appointments regularly. Eventually they offered a trial of another medication and Ellie agreed. This was the game changer. Within a couple of weeks I saw a different girl. She spent time with me because she wanted to, she could speak to me without screaming and seemed calmer and more tolerant to everything and everyone. This medication really gave Ellie a chance to breathe, a chance to think without reacting, and a chance to feel like things were doable and manageable as opposed to overwhelming and stressful. It was amazing! We were advised that these were for short-term use and that Ellie would still need to attend her Cognitive Behavioural Therapy (CBT). The idea was that Ellie would adjust to calmer reactions from a combination of medication and CBT and be able to maintain this after she finished taking the medication. This is what happened for the most part and there were no side effects this time. Ellie took the medication for about two years on and off. As a teen I could only ask her to take it and remind her, rather than be able to give her medicine like when she was small. We still had outbursts, meltdowns and some major issues in school, but these were less frequent. The timing of this medication was completely right for our family, we were at breaking point and this medication was a lifeline.

Would I opt to medicate Alex and Daisy? Thankfully both Alex's and Daisy's needs to-date mean that they haven't needed any medication other than the melatonin Daisy had for about three months when she was three. Both are coping quite well in the grand scheme of things. Meltdowns and outbursts do happen, but not to the same scale as they did with Ellie. And both Daisy and Alex are coping well in school with support and both are doing well socially also. So, it's very much based on the individual needs of your child. If things change going forward and Daisy or Alex are not coping, or we are really struggling to manage challenging behaviours, then I would consider medication in the future. But as with Ellie, I will try lots of other things first. However, if a medical professional advised that medication is needed and that this would be best for my child, then I would absolutely medicate my child.

Stigma

When Daisy was prescribed melatonin (after three years of not sleeping at night and waking 10-20 times throughout the night), I had to bring the consultant's script to be rewritten by my GP. As Daisy was displaying challenging behaviour and was impulsive, the consultant thought that her lack of a full night of sleep may be causing this, or at least not helping the situation. The consultant said we should try the melatonin and see if this had a positive impact on Daisy overall, and regarding her behaviour.

I dropped in the script and waited for a call to say it was ready. Instead a new GP in the surgery called me to discuss my request. She explained that she doesn't prescribe melatonin for children. I was kind of confused ... so I asked to speak to a GP who did. I explained I was asking for a prescription to be rewritten, that it was prescribed by the consultant. The GP then asked me why I would want to medicate my child? Then I realised what was happening. I was being judged. This doctor thought I was wrong to want to give my child medication to help her to sleep. I was blunt. I said Daisy hadn't slept a night since she was born, was displaying challenging behaviour and that I had three other children to care for too. The doctor said she was not comfortable with rewriting the script. I told her I was going to speak to my own GP. I complained (informally) and my GP at that time said some doctors were uncomfortable medicating children. So really as parents we are being judged at every turn or that's how it feels. Thankfully at this time I wasn't especially vulnerable or feeling at the end of my tether, as such an unhelpful judgemental experience could have been the straw that broke the camel's back. I left this GP not long after and have the most wonderful GPs for the last five years. If your GP isn't right for you or your child, please change GPs. GPs are at the forefront and backbone of day-to-day care for autistic children and their parents. You need to have a GP you can talk to and feel understood by.

I do need to mention that side effects of medication for children (usually aimed at increasing attention, decreasing hyperactivity/impulsivity or to reduce violence and aggression) can be pretty horrible. Ellie had heart palpitations on one and considerable weight loss on another. The first one had little effect on behaviour or calming. The second worked well but her teacher reported Ellie was sleepy in school. This is so tough to hear and to see. And you absolutely feel guilt as a parent that you made this choice for your child. And you feel judged by absolutely everybody. But rest in the knowledge that I've yet to meet a parent who medicates their child just because they want to, or because it's the easiest option. Quite the contrary, parents are conflicted, afraid, unsure, hesitant and everything in between before concluding that medication is the right decision for their child.

What the experts say

When I started researching this chapter and all the way through writing I was surprised by how little research there is concerning the stigma around medicating autistic children, or the controversies this presents. And many of the articles I did find which addressed this issue to some extent, are quite dated. Much of the general information I provide below relates to children and medication more generally and specifically pertaining to ADHD, or autism and ADHD combined.

It's important to note that there is no medication for autism, and medication prescribed to autistic children is aimed at symptoms or associated problems which arise for them such as: aggression, hyperactivity, insomnia, or repetitive behaviours.[99] Medication is usually only considered if the child's life is being significantly disrupted by one or a combination of these symptoms. Medication for management of behavioural issues in autistic children is considered to be largely effective in reducing negative and harmful behaviours.[100-102]

A 2021 study concluded autistic children who also have a diagnosis of ADHD are more likely to be taking medication, compared to children with autism alone.[103] Rast and colleagues report that in their review 68% of children with both ASD and ADHD used medication.[103] While only 13% of children with a singular diagnosis of autism used medication. Notably it is estimated that 70% of autistic children also have another comorbid condition.[104]

Brent[105] clarifies that medical professionals themselves take considerable time and evaluate the appropriateness of prescribing medication to a child and whether or not the potential benefits to the child's overall wellbeing are worth the potential risks. Brent further proposes that medication alone is rarely a sufficient treatment plan for a child and is most effective when combined with other therapies.[105]

Sparks and Duncan suggest that parents may feel pressure to medicate their children from professionals and that refusal may be viewed as neglectful parenting.[106] Some professionals advocate that if medication exists to alleviate the negative psychiatric or behavioural symptoms the child is experiencing, then these should be used.

Side effects for medications used for autistic children who also have ADHD include: weight loss, headaches, depression and tics.[107] While LeClerc and Easley[99] add that side effects can be: dizziness, fatigue, changes to appetite, sleep disturbance, gastrointestinal issues and tachycardia (fast heartbeat). Equally, a further ethical debate surrounding medication use for children is that the decision to offer medication is largely based on the views of medical professionals and the constraints in resources of the organisation they work for.[108] For example, budgets will directly impact the availability of behavioural therapies and, consequently, the options for treatment available aside from medication. Mayes and colleagues argue that the wider cultural and societal positions and ideas around the appropriateness of medication for children will substantially impact the physicians in their prescribing of medication based on social norms and acceptability.[108]

Research shows that medication for autistic children aimed at addressing the emotional and behavioural issues discussed, are indeed largely effective.[109] [110] Yet, Politte and colleagues argue that a multifaceted and multi-professional approach to treating emotional and behavioural issues for autistic children is necessary.[111] They further argue that although medications can be effective in targeting some of the behavioural issues the child may be experiencing, that behavioural interventions at the earliest possible time are most helpful to the child in the long term. Examples may include interventions aimed at developing the child's communication or socialisation skills.

KEY LEARNING POINTS FROM THIS CHAPTER:

- Medication is not used to treat autism, but is used to treat some of the symptoms of autism such as repetitive behaviours, challenging or aggressive behaviours or sleep disturbances.
- Autistic children are more likely to be taking medication in cases where there is a second diagnosed condition, such as ADHD.
- Parents often struggle and hesitate in making the decision to try medication for their child.
- Guilt is common for parents who do decide to medicate and the judgement from family, friends and even some professionals, can make this process much more difficult.
- Medication is usually effective in treating autistic children for issues such as aggression, behaviour or sleep.

- Side effects can be pretty horrible for some medications and your child will be monitored closely by their doctor when taking any medication.
- Medication addresses only part of the child's needs, so other interventions and therapies should also be considered.

Conclusion

This chapter gave a whirlwind overview of medication for autistic children. Making the decision to try medication is not something any parent does lightly. The comments and judgement from family and friends around medicating your child can make this decision and process even more difficult. While feelings of guilt (especially if your child suffers side effects) are also common. Although medication for behaviour management usually helps autistic children, this is something which should be discussed in detail with your child's medical team and not something you should feel pressure to agree to. Other therapies should also be considered as part of your plan to support your child in the longer term, on their autism journey.

9

MANAGING CHANGE AND TRANSITIONS

Introduction

The need for sameness is probably one of the few things all three of my autistic children have in common. They need to know what to expect, they need things to stay the same, and anything 'last-minute' causes distress. So for us as a family, to foster calmness and help our children to stay reassured and less anxious, we try to keep things the same, or plan in advance as much as possible when change will occur. At the moment we are building a house. This will be a massive change for both Alex and Daisy who have only ever lived in our current house. So the preparation started before we even broke ground. We drove to the site regularly to let them see where it was, walk around and just feel a bit more familiar with it. We still visit regularly now so they can see the progress and mentally prepare for the move. But it will likely still be very stressful for them and we will need to be extra supportive, continue to do lots of preparation and allow them time and space to process what's happening.

This chapter will explore how difficult changes can be for your autistic child and discuss ways of helping your child to cope with the impact of changes. I will start by sharing experiences with my children around coping with changes and the need for consistency and routine. The momentous move from primary to secondary school will be discussed. This chapter will then look at research surrounding the need for sameness for autistic children and how you can support your child to be better able to cope with and respond to uncertainty.

One of the earliest signs of autism for Daisy was the typical lining up of toys. She once took all the cushions of the couches and lined them from the front door to the back door of our house. But the lining up was quite obsessive. If a toy was moved from the position it was in or she couldn't find it, Daisy would erupt into fits of screaming and nothing but locating this exact toy and putting it back where it should have been would calm her. One day I cleaned Daisy's room. It was an absolute mess (she was about three). So I tidied away all of the toys on the floor and threw out some scraps of paper and rubbish, before sweeping and mopping the floor. When Daisy saw this she completely lost it. It was probably one of the longest and most intense meltdowns she's ever had and lasted for two hours. I felt so guilty. I had done something that made my daughter distraught. We talked through it when Daisy calmed down and I promised I would never, ever do this again. So now when Daisy's room needs to be cleaned, I ask her to help me, or to identify things she doesn't want me to touch. It usually ends up being a negotiation, but it works! And I will never move her things without telling her first.

Changes

Changes cause distress for many children with autism. Changes can be big things like a new sibling in the house or a change of school. But more often they are small things like stopping at the shop on the way to school, or a last-minute/unannounced visitor to our house. These small changes which are unexpected, can still cause distress. And I find that changes can mean your child just doesn't know how to respond. For example, Alex gets his own cereal in the morning. But if the bowls he prefers are not in the cupboard where they usually are, he just won't eat. Or if his lunch in school is in any way different (for example butter on the bread, any meat other than chorizo, or a different container), he will just shut down and not eat. Another example is when I leave Daisy's clothes laid out for her to get dressed. If the shirt is under the pants, or she can't see her cardigan where it should be, this can trigger a meltdown. Alex explains that because the bowl wasn't there, he couldn't get his breakfast. There was no alternative from his perspective. His usual routine was disrupted, and he just couldn't continue. So Alex has a list almost in his head of exactly what to do and what to expect. This helps him to be prepared and feel calm, and certain. When this is disrupted, he abandons the list. It may not make sense to a neuro-typical person, as we might look for an alternative. But for autistic people, they may struggle with considering or committing to an alternative and it can cause major upset and frustration.

Alex is notorious in school for expressing his honest feelings and emotions if a timetable or plan changes at the last minute. Alex struggles a lot with this and finds it extremely difficult to cope with last-minute changes. It can prompt a meltdown or aggressive behaviour. Or it can cause him to be unable to continue as he can't cope with the change. An example would be if a different teacher had the class, if the time of an outing or event changed, or if something is cancelled at the last minute. Alex just can't comprehend an alternative. It's rigid thinking and almost like tunnel vision. It's tough to respond to this and some things are unavoidable and can't be pre-empted. But the things we can influence, we do. We tell Alex in advance what to expect. We tell family members and friends that we need to know things in advance for Alex and that last-minute changes can cause distress.

I still struggle today helping my children to cope with change. I usually start with a low arousal technique, speaking really slowly and calmly. I will always acknowledge how difficult this change is for them. I'm really direct in my communication at times of stress for my child. I'll say: 'I know this is super hard', or 'I'm so sorry that this happened and I can see it has upset you.' Then I'll move on to finding solutions. Such as, 'Well, next time we can try to make sure the start time is what we thought it would be', or 'Okay, I know this isn't what you wanted or what we planned, but how about just for today, we try the other movie/activity/jacket?' I think that my thinking out loud and deliberating is modelling the inner voice focusing on solutions that I want my child to be able to use to reassure themselves. Modelling coping skills and particularly during stressful occurrences is super important (although internally you may feel like screaming!).

We've always encouraged our children to say when they've had enough or are feeling overwhelmed. Daisy is the best at recognising this and letting us know when she needs a break. She uses her noise-cancelling headphones regularly, and has her sleeping mask (an eye mask) for when she's relaxing. And we make a point of hearing them and responding positively when they tell us they are overwhelmed. Daisy will say 'I just need a break', or 'this is just too much for me'. And when she does, we stop doing what we're doing (usually homework) and take a break. This is a skill and resource we as adults would love to have, so I'm exceptionally proud of the little person Daisy is becoming.

Prompting your child to react differently is also helpful. Acknowledging what happened: 'Okay, the bowls are not there. What could you do to eat breakfast? Where could the bowls be?' Staying with them in that moment, but without judgement and offering supportive solutions, can help.

New shoes and clothes can also cause upset for your child. Daisy would refuse point blank (and still does) to wear certain new clothes, so we return them or end up giving them away. Letting her choose things herself (usually online) helps. Alex has a massive issue with shoes. He will wear one pair and one pair only. He won't wear new shoes and we have, in the past, bought the same pair in the next size up so that he is more comfortable. We have also 'misplaced' his old shoes, so he will try the new ones. We always keep the brand the same, so the look and feel of them is familiar to him and reduces some of the distress caused by the change.

Other changes which have impacted my children have been: change of our family car, going on holidays (and what to expect), visiting places we haven't been to before and even when Granny moved house. We are learning all the time about what can cause upset and, therefore, we have become much better at pre-empting changes and helping to prepare for these. But more than anything else, accepting your child where they are with difficulty in coping with uncertainty is key. I won't ever try to change my child. I will only try to improve their ability to cope with the difficulties and challenges they face.

The move from primary to secondary school

This is a time I've worried about so much since our first child was diagnosed with autism, so it's something I think is really important to discuss within managing changes and transitions. I've had two completely different experiences with this massive transition. For Ellie, it was by far the most distressing and completely overwhelming experience of her young life. She was absolutely terrified, confused, shocked … she really struggled with this transition. She called me every day for the first two weeks crying and begging me to collect her and bring her home. I did one or two days, but other days I said no and then spent the rest of the day crying when I got off the phone. It was horrible and I felt like I was doing this to her. That I had the power to not make her go through this and let her stay home.

I was in to the school so much in those first few months. And we were so lucky that the school was doing everything they could to support Ellie with this major transition and reduce some of the distress she felt. Some of the specific issues Ellie struggled with:

- Organising books between classes
- Understanding and following the timetable
- Queueing in the canteen at lunch time was too much (pushing and shoving, too many people, etc.)
- The crowds and proximity of other people when moving from class to class

As this school was known for being established in supporting students with additional needs they came up with solutions for most of these issues. They colour-coded Ellie's books and timetable to enable her to get a better grip on this. They had an SNA help Ellie at her locker with organising her books and stationery for the day. They allowed her to leave class five minutes early to go to the canteen before crowds and queues started. These strategies really helped and although Ellie never loved school, she managed and coped well overall.

So after such a horrendous experience with Ellie, I was very anxious in the year before Alex was due to start secondary school.

I tried to be as proactive as I could to reduce the distress he might feel with the move. Both Alex's amazing Sixth Class teacher, his resource teacher and his service providers worked really hard to prepare Alex for moving schools. However, the Covid pandemic hit so many of the plans to visit the school in the final few months of primary school couldn't happen. But the secondary school was fantastic and arranged some pre-visits for all of the kids with additional needs. This was extremely helpful and I would urge all schools and parents to make sure this happens. Equally, the open evening for the school was really different and inclusive, and Alex absolutely loved it. So when he started in First Year I was a bag of nerves and on edge waiting for the phone to ring ... but it didn't. Alex adapted to secondary school well. He was absolutely fine. Some of the things he found tough were following his timetable and organising his notebooks. But upon communicating this to the school, they immediately put mechanisms in place to help him. This was reassuring for him also and sent a clear message that if something is difficult and he tells his parents or teachers, we can help and things will get better. Now there are some parts of school that Alex doesn't like such as group work or answering a question in class. But his school and the staff are patient and provide a real individual, student-focused learning environment where they identify the child's strengths and build on these. And it really, *really* works.

What the experts say

Rydzewska states that autistic people can find adjusting to transitions or unexpected changes in their routine as complicated.[112] According to the American Psychiatric Association,[7] this rigid need for routine and predictability, combined with a reduced capacity to cope when things change, are typical symptoms of autism. Change for a child with autism can be 'fraught with anxiety' and can lead to feelings of fear and major distress.[113] When the child is perhaps unable to express these feelings, they may display challenging behaviour or experience a meltdown.[113]

A need for sameness and certainty can result in children with autism becoming fixated on routines and knowing exactly what to expect.[114] Such strict adherence to routines and sameness means that some children don't get to experience new situations and their development and maturity may be limited because of this.[114] An example of this might be a child in their early teens going to the cinema with friends and without adult supervision, or a teen getting the bus alone. However, the risks versus the benefits for a child with autism may mean that their parents decide this is not safe for them, or the risk of something unexpected happening and their child being unable to cope with this are too high. So they may avoid trying new things and experiences as a means of protection. Equally, if a child with autism has always visited the cinema with a parent, veering away from this for a new experience may be something they will resist.

Rigid thinking and a need for things to stay exactly the same, are common features of ASD.[115] Rajendran and Mitchell[116] argue that autism causes difficulties with cognitive flexibility, so the child can feel unable to react and think of alternatives or solutions. Ionescu[117] finds that people need to navigate cognitions between the context and environment that they are in, and with the task or problem presented, in order to demonstrate cognitive flexibility successfully. Ritualistic behaviour is further common in children with autism in their attempts to keep things the same and increase certainty in what will happen. Ritualistic behaviour is when your child follows a specific sequence or routine when completing tasks but obsessively or compulsively so. Brooks and colleagues[118] define ritualistic behaviour as 'a fixed sequence of behaviours that are often characterized by formality and repetition'. Rituals mean that things have to be in exactly the same order or sequence all the time, and variation from this can result in the child's inability to proceed.[119] Children with autism often describe things as right or wrong. If it's right, it's the way it's meant to be according to their ritual. This could relate to the order in which clothes are put on or taken off. For Alex, when I leave his clothes out they must be laid in a certain order (underwear and socks on top, then t-shirt, jumper and trousers). If they're not like this or exactly how he expects them to be, then they're not right.

Another way of describing the challenges children with autism experience when coping with change is intolerance of uncertainty.[120] Rodgers and colleagues argue that intolerance of uncertainty decreases potential anxiety.[121] So creating interventions to increase tolerance for uncertainty, as opposed to attempting to increase certainty, is an effective method of reducing anxiety. The CUES programme (Coping with Uncertainty in Everyday Situations) focuses on: offering choices, planning for the unexpected and talking through difficult situations with your child.[121] Repetitive behaviours can be used as a coping mechanism for anxiety due to uncertainty, or anxiety can trigger repetitive behaviours.[122] The CUES programme involves parent training and support, combined with emotional literacy skills for parents and children.

One interesting study found that intolerance for uncertainty was even higher for children with greater communication difficulties, or repetitive behaviours.[123] Therefore, children who struggle most with uncertainty, are already likely to be struggling with other aspects of living with autism.[123] Navigating interactions with other people and daily routines is challenging for people with autism, if no change happens. So when an unexpected change happens, the child must interpret, process and respond to this change, while simultaneously trying to decipher and cope with the environment they are in.[122]

Cumming and colleagues argue that planning can substantially alleviate some of the distress children with autism experience at times of major transition.[124] Both formal planning with the child in school or within healthcare services combined with more informal planning and discussion with family, is more likely to be an effective method of support.[124]

Parents and teachers can support children to cope with changes and transitions by identifying the needs and preferences of the child and building support mechanisms around this.[125] For example, if we know a child loves art, or playing computer games, these preferences could be incorporated when helping them to adjust to unplanned changes or difficult transitions. The timing of introducing a change can impact the response.[115] Therefore, choosing a time where the child appears calm, or is coping well, as opposed to a time when they are exhibiting stress or sensory overload, is preferable. Register and Humpal report a unique way of supporting autistic children to adjust to transitions in their routine with the use of music.[126] Their research found that pre-planned songs at intervals throughout the school day to signify a transition or change in task were effective in helping children to make these transitions more easily.

So what can you do to help your child to cope with change?

Teaching your child relaxation and calming skills prior to a change in routine or an unexpected situation, will equip them with the skills to better cope.[127] Hume and colleagues suggest that using a calming app with headphones, watching a favourite show on TV or doing slow breathing exercises, are ideal ways to help your child to relax.[127] When doing these calming activities becomes habit or routine for your child, they will be able to use these when a change or transition happens.

Barton and Harn state that planning based on the individual child and their unique needs is essential to support children with navigating transitions.[128] Equally as important is working in partnership between the child, parents, teachers and other professionals involved in their care. If everyone communicates and works towards the same goal, the support your child receives will be consistent and will be more likely to be successful.[128] An example of this type of collaboration might be preparing your child to move from pre-school to primary school. Collaboration between pre-school teachers and primary-school staff (teacher, SNA and resource teacher) will help to prepare the child within each of the classroom settings. Guidance should be sought from your child's doctor, OT, SLT, etc. regarding how best to communicate the expected changes to your child, and how you can best prepare them for this transition.

Wright and Williams suggest that reflecting on a situation or incident with your child afterwards, and discussing this, can help them to cope better if faced with the same situation again.[129] They suggest asking your child to write down or draw a picture of what happened, then explore with them how they responded, how they felt and how they might have responded differently. An example might be lashing out or hurting you or their sibling when they feel overwhelmed with an unexpected change. So later, when things have calmed down, you would review what happened with them asking questions such as: 'What other way could you have shown me you were sad?' 'What might have been a more helpful way to act?' 'What will you do if this happens again?'

KEY LEARNING POINTS FROM THIS CHAPTER:

- Change and transitions (especially unplanned) often cause distress and anxiety for children with autism.
- Needing sameness and an intolerance of uncertainty are key symptoms of autism.
- Life transitions like starting school or moving to secondary school can be a period of substantial change for an autistic child.
- Planning and collaborating with teachers and healthcare providers can help your child to make transitions less upsetting and traumatic.
- Using methods to enhance your child's ability to adapt and cope with changes and transitions will help them to feel less distressed when faced with transitions.
- Try relaxation techniques when your child is calm to help them to adjust when they feel the anxiety that change may bring.
- You can use reflection and discussion with your child after an incident where they struggled with change, and use this to explore better ways they could respond in the future.

Conclusion

This chapter has introduced the topic of changes and transitions and how tough they can be for autistic children. This is something that your child will likely continue to struggle with as they get older, so finding strategies to help them is equipping them with the tools to cope with changes when they happen. Transitions can cause substantial anxiety for autistic children and this may increase repetitive behaviours as your child tries to cope. Through collaboration with your child's teachers and professionals involved in their care you can work to create strategies based on your child's individual needs to support them to adjust and cope with transitions.

10

IMPACT ON YOUR FAMILY

Introduction

Autism isn't something that affects your child. Autism is *part of* your child and, consequently, will be part of your whole family. Accepting this and adjusting to this will make each day and each challenge you experience a little easier to cope with. This chapter will explore the impact of having an autistic child on your family as a whole. Seeing your autistic child struggle and planning to meet their needs impacts most decisions you make as a parent and, consequently, your family life. A child with autism requires more attention and support than neurotypical children. How to cope overall as a family will be discussed in addition to practical ways of helping your family and other children to adjust to autism and how this will affect their lives.

My experience

An 'autism mom' is something I've referred to myself as and I think this title accurately represents autism in my life. However, many autistic adults on social media platforms have expressed dissatisfaction with 'autism moms' calling themselves this, as they aren't themselves autistic. There's lots of negativity surrounding this label and a lot of hate directed towards parents of autistic children online. Yet I still feel this label most accurately reflects me in my role as a mother of three autistic children. I don't have autism. But autism affects every single aspect of my life. It's part of my three children, it impacts decisions we make, school, social life, mental well-being – absolutely everything. I've immersed myself in autism and read everything I can. It's my normal, it's my every day and my everything. Autism is part of my family, it's a massive part of my life and will be forever. I feel this is a part of my identity as a mother and is something I consider first and foremost when planning anything or making any major decision. I can't emotionally or practically detach myself from autism, as this would mean detaching myself from my children and their needs. They can't always identify their own needs, or articulate these. They aren't always able to advocate for themselves and will possibly need support to navigate the world through their adult lives. So I need to be an 'autism mom', they need me to be their everything, their hope, their advocate, their supporter and the person who would fiercely defend them no matter what. I don't want to offend an autistic person with this name, however. An 'autism mom' (which essentially means 'a mom of an autistic child/children') is my choice for what I call myself, and this is my preference and what I believe to be the most fitting description of who I am. I'm intrinsically linked to my children, they lived in my body before they were born (I tell them this all the time: 'You know where you used to live?'), and their needs are needs I feel responsible for meeting. So we're enmeshed as people and always will be.

As a family, when we are planning a social event or have a family occasion we have to consider and remain mindful of how our children will cope with this. Consequently, autism can impact our whole family socially. We attended a friend's child's first holy communion recently. The anxiety in the days before was really visible for Alex and Daisy. 'What time will it be at?', 'Who will be there?', 'What will we do?', 'Where will I sit?' And the uncertainty is really tough for both of them to take. On the morning of the communion, Alex said over and over again that he didn't want to go, and asked why did he have to go. Daisy asked from 9.00 a.m. until we left at 2.00 p.m., to go to the party, what time it would be at and how long more there was until we would leave. This is Daisy's way of getting more certainty about what will happen and feeling more prepared. When we got there both Daisy and Alex were subdued but managing. With some prompting Daisy went to play with the other kids. But Alex stayed close to us. He was stimming quite a lot (rocking) but seemed to be coping quite well, given the busy environment. A few friends tried to speak to him and he replied sometimes with an: 'Mmm hhmmm', or 'Yes now'. Friends asked if he was okay. I explained that he was fine. Stimming can worry other people when they don't understand it. But for Alex it was comforting him in a situation he found overwhelming. After an hour Alex moved away from us to sit on his own in the corner. Initially he sat on the floor. I brought over a chair for him to sit on and checked that he was okay. He asked if it was time to go home. I said 'Yes we will be leaving soon.' Not long after, music was put on a loudspeaker and that was it. Alex said 'We need to leave. It's too loud.' And he began pacing over and back. I knew he had reached his limit and we needed to leave. So I started saying my goodbyes and Alex got more and more worked up. He told me that I'd said we were leaving but we didn't, we were still here (a fair point). As we left Alex complained all the way home about the noise and how long it took us to leave. We gave Alex the space to express himself and agreed that it was noisy, and we should have left sooner. Alex seemed okay with this and we moved on with our day. Our family is impacted by autism. Autism sometimes negatively affects my children. So we have to react and respond when this happens and try to offset this negative impact and try to make our children feel better.

In my family, Daisy calls Daniel the 'adopted' one, as he is the only child in our family without an autism diagnosis. This is hard for Daniel. He asked me once when he was little why he didn't have any appointments. This really struck me. Daniel saw Ellie and Alex attending appointments sometimes twice a week, and I would have meetings in their school, or we would be juggling schedules to keep up with therapies. It never occurred to me that Daniel really noticed, but he did. Daniel has always been so kind, caring, genuine and protective of Ellie. When Ellie was acting out, or even when she hurt him when they were small, Daniel would try to defend Ellie and get her out of trouble. He would make excuses for her behaviour and even mediated between Ellie and me when things were super difficult. We have always tried to spend some one-to-one time with

Daniel, so that he knows that he is just as important to us as his siblings are. He has always accepted that his siblings' needs often supersede his, so making the time we do have with Daniel count is important. I always tell him how proud I am of him and exactly why. I think it's so important that we let him know how much we love him and how much he matters to us.

Another major challenge in parenting three autistic and one neurotypical child is the boundaries and rules which vary considerably from one child to the other. Ellie and Daniel being so close in age really highlighted this for me. Ellie could hit me, smash a cup and refuse to tidy her room, all in the same day. But if Daniel so much as muttered under his breath, I would pull him up on it. He would often ask why Ellie didn't get in to trouble for something, but he did? It's a fair question and comes up now with Alex and Daisy. When your child finds managing their emotions and behaviour so difficult and when they are acting out maybe twenty times in one day, you simply can't punish them and follow through with this every time. If I were to react to my autistic children the same way as I would with Daniel, they would be having consequences most of the time. One of the best pieces of advice I got from a professional was choosing behaviours to ignore. Initially this sounded crazy to me! If Daisy curses or throws something at me, I should ignore it? But after trying it, I realised it worked. So we ignored bad language with Ellie, we ignored screaming with Daisy (when she did it out of anger). And it meant they weren't constantly being reprimanded and often it diffused challenging behaviour much more quickly. But then Daniel had to see this and have a completely different set of rules for his behaviour. He still says it's not fair... and he's right. We have to be more flexible with the boundaries and our expectations for our autistic children, based on their unique needs and challenges. Whereas our expectations for Daniel concerning his behaviour are different. We want all of our children to behave well and be kind always to other people. But addressing each incident of bad behaviour for a child who struggles to 'behave well' for hours on end, just isn't going to help them in the long run. Instead we praise good behaviour, we remind all of our children how very proud of them we are, and for exactly what.

In my effort to help my children and when Ellie was pre-diagnosis, I attended a parenting course. I felt, like many parents do, that this suggested that my child's behavioural or emotional issues were my fault. When the parenting course is the first thing they offer you when you think your child might have autism ... it hurts. Anyway, I attended and it was actually really helpful. So they suggested 'catching your child being good'. So basically you stop and take the time to tell your child their behaviour is really good, and exactly why. The same way you would if the behaviour was bad or harmful. This was a game changer. Rather than always correcting or reprimanding, I was saying: 'Well done, you're playing so nicely!' Or 'Good job for speaking in a nice, calm voice.' It also made me feel like I was a better parent and that my communication with my kids wasn't always negative.

Autism impacts every single aspect of our lives as a family. Any time we plan to go anywhere, the meals we eat and the timing of our day/routine means we as parents are constantly pre-empting our children's needs and trying to prepare for every eventuality to make things less stressful for them. For example, we were invited for a BBQ at a relative's house recently. It was last minute (a same-day invite) so we had to say no. We hadn't prepared the kids for this and telling them with a couple of hours' notice just wouldn't work.

On one occasion I picked Daisy and Alex up from Granny's and I could tell immediately that we were in for a tough evening. Daisy was super cranky and agitated and going out of her way to annoy Alex and me intentionally. She threw her clothes, one item at a time, all over the kitchen and kept going into the sitting room where Alex was doing his homework, trying to tease him and get him to react. I gave her warning number 1 ... 'If you don't stop misbehaving, you will have no TV time tonight.' Within 10 minutes she had done the same thing three more times. So I said: 'Now you have no TV and it's bedtime'. (It really was bedtime.) She threw a shoe at me, used every curse word she had ever heard, and slammed each door as she banged her way up the stairs. She came down four more times, banged the doors twice more ... and used a few more curse words.

How do events like this impact us as a family? Alex is tired after being in school all day. He wants to do his homework and wants to be left alone and for Daisy not to go near him. My husband and I are stressed, tired and on edge when the challenging behaviour is persisting. We are snappy with one another and the feeling overall in the house is pretty awful. Everyone feels it. Daisy feels it too. I feel anxious and am waiting for things to kick off again. The atmosphere in the whole house is stressful.

*Note: After the events above, Daisy wrote a sorry card and sent it down the stairs. It said sorry and had a list of requests for things she would like us to bring upstairs (books, a drink and a response straight away). It took two more hours of Daisy coming down the stairs every five minutes asking if she could come down, if she could have a drink, if we could we help her find something. She asked questions like: do we not love her? She says she can't fall asleep, she's too hot, she's bored. She flits between pleading and screaming, using bad language and banging doors again. It is absolutely exhausting, and it feels like the whole evening is written off. We're consistent in our responses but the temptation to give in and let her have the TV time, or to come back downstairs for a while, is there. We take turns responding to her and we try to be patient, fair but firm. But it's hard!

On the flip side, when Daisy initiates a hug – it's a hug like no other. She really, really means it and you can feel this in the hug. She's completely present and giving her full self to the hug. Daisy is so snuggly and is my best snuggler in the house. She loves having her back and head massaged. She also loves having her head scratched. So, when Daisy is getting worked up, an offer of a back massage can help her to regulate herself and feel better.

At this stage, it would be interesting to get my husband's take on this too wouldn't it?! Parenting a child with additional learning needs can be stressful. Parenting three children with autism is definitely challenging. I am a bag of stress at times and I often feel overwhelmed with the responsibility of it all. By choice and due to the fact that I am a control freak, I have always managed the children's assessments, therapies, appointments, school meetings and everything else. I delegate to their Dad sometimes, but for the most part I insist on doing it all myself. I think that as mothers we feel this immense pressure to be perfect, to balance it all and to be everything to everyone. People ask me how I do it. I do it because

I want to and because I have to. On the very rare occasions where I have delegated an appointment or parent–teacher meeting to my husband, it has caused arguments every time. I have given him a list (I know ... see this is part of the problem) and if he hasn't discussed things I wanted him to bring up, or asked a question I wanted to ask, then I'm not satisfied. Equally, when I ask how it went he generally says: 'Fine.' So I prefer doing these things myself. I end up doing the meetings 99% of the time and then end up complaining about how busy and stressed I am. But this is just how we operate. And it's great when my husband can attend too, but his work as a plumber means that this is rarely possible for us.

On a really busy day, if I've got a call from the school, or there's a club and an appointment on and I am at work, I do find myself being less patient and more snappy in my interactions with my husband. I think that sometimes on a tough day I blame him. It makes absolutely no sense, I know! But if I'm stressed, I sometimes feel he should be too, which isn't logical. He is a very, very relaxed and patient husband and Dad, so thankfully his calm approach usually reduces the stress and once I have had a chance to get things out of my system (and have a bit of a rant), things are generally okay again. This is just what works for us. But the breaks we get without the kids have really been the saving grace of our relationship with one another. It's easy to become completely consumed with parenting and autism, it's a full-time job. So making time for our own relationship is essential. If we're putting on a united front and communicating well, supporting each other and feeling happy in our marriage, we will be more effective parents. This is the ideal, I know. Not every family has the luxury of respite and support. But this is what works for us.

What the experts say

The financial implications of having an autistic child have been widely reported on.[130-132] One large scale study in Latin America with 2,942 families participating, found that 47% of families had to reduce the number of hours they worked. While 35% of families had to stop working altogether because of the impact of their child's autism diagnosis.[131] Roddy and O'Neill[133] in their Irish study report that many families with autistic children pay for therapies and assessments privately, which places an additional financial burden on them. Interesting, Roddy and O'Neill found that the more severe the autism, the higher the expenditure and financial burden the family are likely to experience. While another study suggests that sociodemographic differences can be found in out-of-pocket expenditure associated with autism.[134] One study found that lower income families and families with a lower level of education spend less on therapies, while higher-income families and those with a greater level of education, tend to spend more.[134] This suggests that spending on therapies and intervention for some families is based largely on the availability of money to pay for this, or a greater insight perhaps regarding the need and benefits of therapy, due to academic achievement. These findings really emphasise the ongoing disadvantage and adversity experienced by some families and highlight even more so the need for state supports and therapies for children with autism.

I can relate to these findings based on my own experiences. We must have had ten or more childminders over a three-year period when Ellie was small. Her challenging behaviour meant that childminders were unable to cope with her needs. So my working hours reduced substantially as we could not source and maintain appropriate childcare. Equally, any day of the week could mean a phone call from school. Flexibility in my job and working hours mean I can leave if I need to. But many jobs don't provide this flexibility.

It is widely accepted that having a child with autism places increased pressure and stress on parental relationships.[135] [136] Chan and Leung report that marital conflict is increased for parents of autistic children. Most of the literature refers to married parents (which is limiting and perhaps assuming).[135] But the evidence discussed here is applicable to anyone cohabiting or co-parenting, regardless of marital status.

Substantial differences have been identified between a mother's and father's perceptions regarding their child's autism.[137] Grebe and colleagues report that mothers suffer from greater stress relating to their child's autism compared to fathers and this may be due to the proximity of care with mothers often undertaking a primary-care role.[137] It has further been suggested that, spill-over of parental stress can result in marital/relationship stress for parents.[138] The level of parental stress experienced (e.g. in response to challenging behaviour) can reduce the likelihood of positive interactions between both parents. This is certainly evident in my family. On really stressful days, interactions between myself and my husband are strained and there may be a day where our only communication is stress driven and aimed at managing multiple competing demands or challenging behaviour.

Interventions which aim to empower parents to respond to the symptoms of autism can have a positive effect on the co-parenting relationship.[135] Mothers tend to have more parenting responsibility according to Foody, James and Leader.[138] I do think this is partly due to societal pressure on mothers to provide the caring role, while fathers have greater expectations placed on them concerning work and providing roles. Green proposes that all family members are affected and adjust to cope with the needs of an autistic child.[139] As siblings grow and mature together, neurotypical children become more aware of their sibling's inability to control their behaviour at times and develop more tolerance for this as they age. Siblings can feel an additional sense of responsibility to their autistic sibling and will often take on the role of caregiver.[140] Some children will act in a protective capacity and feel they should defend their sibling if they are being picked on or excluded.[140]

Many families are impacted negatively when much-needed supports and resources are unavailable.[141] Kovshoff and colleagues report that the supports and services available to families, or lack thereof, further affect all members of the family.[141] For example, if parents chose not to access formal support services or engage with therapies, or if one or both parents are unwilling to accept a diagnosis of autism for their child. The reaction and engagement of the family with available supports substantially impacts their coping and adjustment to autism and the challenges that come with this.

KEY LEARNING POINTS FROM THIS CHAPTER

- Autism affects each member of the family, not just those with a diagnosis.
- Autism can impact families financially, with availability to work being an issue and due to paying for therapies and assessments.

- Siblings are usually substantially affected by having an autistic brother or sister. Making time to connect with them and really discuss their needs is really important.
- Varying rules for your children (based on their unique needs) can create upset and challenges. Open discussion and space for asking questions is key.
- The challenges that arise in parenting an autistic child can put strain on a relationship or marriage. The additional attention required to care for a child with additional needs can result in conflict between parents and high stress levels.
- Insufficient family support and a lack of therapies and services can make the challenges experienced by autistic children even more difficult.

Conclusion

This chapter explained some of the everyday challenges we experience as a family in navigating autism and how this affects our children. Coping with challenging behaviour and caring for more than one child can feel really difficult some days, and that's with the fantastic family support we are lucky enough to have (with Granny). Having children with additional needs can be stressful for parental relationships. Neurotypical siblings and other siblings with autism can be triggered and upset by one another. As parents, spending even a little time with each child on their own can be beneficial and having an environment where we can talk about our difficulties together helps. Respite has been the difference between sinking and swimming on this journey for us as a family. Yet I'm all too aware that there are families out there who don't get respite.

11

COPING WHEN YOU'RE NOT COPING

Introduction

This chapter will look at the challenges of coping as a parent of an autistic child. Coping … or not coping can be like the elephant in the room. As parents, and as mothers, we often feel like we should cope and that feeling as though we can't cope, is because something is wrong with us or with how we're parenting. I can tell you that feeling like you're not coping, is a completely normal part of the journey as a parent of an autistic child. The key is ensuring that this is a short-term feeling only and that you have the power to impact and change this.

This chapter will discuss, honestly, my experiences of struggling to cope with parenting. This chapter will examine ways that you can increase your coping capacity and look at what to do when you're really not coping. What the experts say regarding parental stress and coping when parenting an autistic child will further be explored.

My experiences

I've felt like I'm not coping well more times than I can count. I've had days where I've stayed in bed, nights when I couldn't sleep and days when everything made me cry. When I feel overwhelmed with parenting, appointments, assessments and challenging behaviour, everything can seem insurmountable. And then the cycle of negative occurrences happens. When I feel overwhelmed every task feels like I'm climbing a mountain. Even cooking a dinner or doing homework with the kids can seem like it's just too much. I'm snappy with my children and less able to respond calmly when they have sensory overload and need me to put on their sock for the seventh time or when they are arguing simply because one is breathing on the other.

I know I'm coping less well when everything irritates me. When being called 'Mom Mom Mom Mom Mom Mom Mom...' is something I just can't listen to one more time.

One day we had planned to drive to Roscommon with our smaller two, Alex and Daisy. I had clothes prepared the night before, spare clothes, colouring books and small toys for the car (it's an hour-long journey) and plenty of snacks. I could feel myself stressed in the build up to the journey so, in hindsight, we should have cancelled. But when I feel like I can't manage something, it often makes me feel like I need to prove to myself that I can. Anyway, Daisy was not playing ball that morning. If I put on a shoe, she kicked it off. If I brushed her hair she would run and scream and intentionally mess up her hair again. It took hours to get ready and Daisy had hit me and hit Alex by the time we got to the car. I was snapping at my husband and could pretty much foresee that it was going to be a very long day.

The hour-long journey started with Alex kicking my seat, repeatedly. Daisy was spitting food at Alex and he was repeating the same thing again and again and again. I unstrapped my seatbelt probably six times on the way there to separate the kids, give them snacks, clean spills and basically prevent them from almost killing each other. By the time we arrived to visit my husband's family I felt as if I had been awake for 48 hours. So at this point (as I had threatened so many times on route!), we should have admitted defeat and gone home. But this made me think about how 'bad' a parent I was, how I couldn't even manage an hour-long car journey with only two of my children, and how very different my family was. This made me question my parenting: 'What was I doing wrong? What were we doing wrong?' We did make it to my husband's family for our planned visit. I was on edge the whole time, waiting for more challenges or the kids to start having a go at each other again. The visit, however, was quite eventless. An hour (and lots of lovely food and treats) later the children had been super calm and well behaved and we headed for home. But by the time we reached our house I was sobbing. The trip home was as difficult as the trip there. We swore there and then that we wouldn't be doing any more long drives.

This car journey experience is our norm, unfortunately. Since Ellie was born and even now with Daisy and Alex being eight and fourteen, long car journeys (more than a half an hour), just don't work for our family. This means we haven't visited my husband's family in Roscommon in quite a while. And we have to say no when invited to events or days out that are far away. It's just not worth the stress or upset for the children and for us.

So what do I do?

Sometimes I declare a 'STOP' day. When things get too much for one of my children, if challenging behaviour is overwhelming or if a cycle of negative interactions and crises become more frequent, we just take a day out. A STOP day has to be whatever works for you and your family. What makes you relaxed? It could involve no cleaning and no cooking, getting a takeaway, having a pyjama day or having some tablet or gaming time. It's a day where your child feels no pressure and, as a result, this has a calming effect on the whole family. The key principles of a STOP day are illustrated in the figure on page 118.

Sometimes, I have to be really disciplined with myself in order to move my mindset from negative and overwhelmed to capable and determined. My internal monologue can be really damaging when I feel overwhelmed. If I tell myself 'I can't cope', 'This is all too much', 'I can't do this' or 'I'm a bad parent', this is what I will believe. And on the bad days, these things do go through my head. But I help myself change my internal dialogue, as no one else can do this apart from me. My husband and friends can tell me what a great job I'm doing, how well my kids are doing, but unless I tell myself, it won't sink in. So I have created mantras for myself that I repeat over and over again on the days that are really hard to cope with. I tell myself: 'You can do this!', 'You're a good parent', 'Your children are amazing!', and 'Things will be 100% okay.'

Figure 11.1 What is a STOP Day?

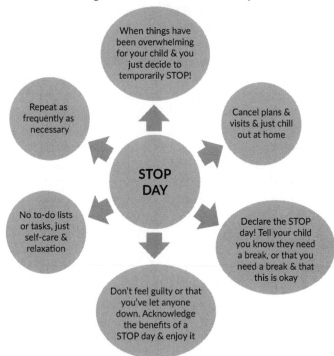

Daisy was six years old and was really excited about Halloween. She had had a party in school and then would have a week of holidays before Halloween night. During that week, however, Daisy's behaviour gradually got more and more challenging. Her tolerance for everything was decreased and she started screaming, hitting us and throwing things every day. I couldn't put the pieces together and work out the cause at the time. But finally, I realised it was Halloween. The build-up was too much. The impending excitement was creating anxiety for her and she was unable to understand this or to express it verbally. So she was lashing out. I employed all of my usual techniques at the time but none worked. The challenging behaviour was started to feel insurmountable. We had two events planned at the weekend. The first was a party for Daniel and the second was attending a friend's christening. On the morning of Daniel's birthday, we had gone out for a meal. Daisy's behaviour during the meal was absolutely uncontrollable. She was grabbing cake, spitting food and shouting loudly in the restaurant. I could feel my

stress levels rising and this was making me less able to respond calmly and maintain control. When we got home from the restaurant I made the decision that we were going to have a stop day. We cancelled our plans to attend the christening in the afternoon and explained to the children that we were going to just chill out. Daisy asked lots of questions and I answered honestly. I told her that her behaviour was very hard to cope with, and acknowledged that she wasn't feeling good or calm and we all just needed to stay at home and have an easy day instead. The relief for both of us was almost immediate. I felt the tension in my chest ease and I felt like we all could just breathe.

Now when an event or holiday is coming up and Daisy is becoming anxious, we plan in advance exactly what we will do on that day and even at what time. So for Halloween we went to Auntie Fiona's. We told Daisy exactly what would happen for the whole evening and offered her repeated reassurance. We explained as often as she needed in the run-up to this (which was very often) exactly what the day would look like and what would happen. This didn't get rid of Dasiy's anxiety completely, but it definitely helped her to feel more certain of what to expect, and less worried about uncertainties.

Sometimes then, in the middle of a particularly tough day, Daisy will say or do something that just changes everything. Daisy gives compliments only when she absolutely wholeheartedly means it. So, when Daisy says 'Mom, that dress is so pretty', or 'Dad, you look so handsome', we completely melt. Because Daisy doesn't do fake or say what's expected of her to say. Daisy does only honest and only real. So when you get a compliment, it's the best! And she has me in stitches with her wicked sense of humour where she maintains her absolute honesty – she really is is the funniest little person. Daisy draws pictures of Granny and Auntie Maureen as *very* old people with walking sticks and glasses (they're in their 60s). She writes the most amazing songs and poems, and really detailed and elaborate stories. She's so authentic and unapologetically herself, it's mesmerising. When Covid started, she said, 'well if Grandad gets it he's a gonner, cause he's so old!' So even when I do feel like I'm struggling to cope and feel overwhelmed with the weight of everything, a one-liner from Daisy can give me a much-needed giggle.

Self-care

Self-care is not a luxury, it's a necessity for parents of autistic children. If I don't invest in self-care, I can't be my best in supporting and caring for my children. There's been many days where I've felt like not doing my self-care activities, where I'd prefer to have a glass of wine or to go to bed. But I make myself, because I deserve care, and my children need me to be well in order to care for them to the best of my ability.

First of all, my self-care activities might look like your worst nightmare! So although this is what I do, this might not work for you. I started doing Yoga a few years ago, not thinking that it would be my cup of tea. But it turned out that I really loved it. Focusing on the poses takes so much concentration and energy that it clears my mind of everything else. And I'm much less stressed after it and I also sleep better. Meeting with friends or having a night out have gradually interested me less over the last few years (the pandemic didn't help!). But when I do make the effort to go out for dinner, or meet up with friends for a drink, I realise how much I needed it and how nice it feels. Whenever I meet up with friends, for the time I'm with them I'm not anyone's mom. I don't have to do anything, I can just 'be'. My responsibilities (which feel overwhelming at times) are temporarily suspended. This is so nice and so necessary. And if your friends are people who fill your cup and really make you feel good, then these are the people you need to spend time with.

Going for a walk with my headphones and listening to some podcast or watching a YouTube video is another easy way to take a breather when things are tough. Again I'm focusing on the story I'm listening to, or where I'm walking in the woods. And for this short time I'm alone and not responsible for anyone. When I get back I feel refreshed and I have the feeling that 'I can do this!' I love gym classes too. I find it hard to motivate myself to really exercise, so the classes mean I have to push myself and it's a social opportunity too. When I feel healthy in my body, my mind feels healthier and my coping capacity increases. I owe this investment in myself to myself. I deserve to be well and to feel well. And I know that when I feel good, everything is easier. I feel more confident in my parenting, I know I can cope when things get difficult and that I can respond in the ways that I want to in order to meet my child's needs. If I'm stressed or not coping, a fight between the kids can feel insurmountable. But when I've invested in my self-care and I feel good, I can deescalate an argument between my children effectively, without feeling overwhelmed.

Asking for help

The most important skill I have developed in relation to coping when I feel like I'm not coping, is knowing when to ask for help, and knowing where to go. This is very, very difficult. I used to feel like asking for help as a parent was admitting defeat or saying that I'm failing and can't manage my own family. Slowly I realised that asking for help is the difference between feeling like your sinking and feeling like you're swimming. Where do I go for help? Knowing exactly what I need helps to guide me with where to go for help. If I need respite, I will ask a family member (usually Granny) to help. Even having asked her, it eases some of the stress and pressure straight away. If I need to talk about how I'm feeling or if I'm struggling, I have different friends for different things. If I need a hug and a cup of tea I'll go to one friend, or if I need someone to say: 'Suck it up and get on with things', I'll go to another friend. I have also found that going online and chatting to other moms can be the kindest most empathetic place to go for support, and I'm so grateful for this!

If I'm really struggling, identifying this is key. If I don't, things will be more challenging for my children and my husband, so keeping myself well is fundamental to the wellbeing of my entire family (no pressure!). In this instance, I go to my GP. I have said already in this book how truly blessed I am to have an amazing GP. And just knowing I have this support there, is really comforting and reassuring in itself. I've also found that attending counselling sessions regularly helps me to keep on top of how I'm feeling and how I'm coping. Having an external person to bounce things off and get impartial advice from or tips for reflection, has been instrumental on my journey with my autistic children. Counselling helps to keep me feeling well and feeling capable, as opposed to fixing things when they become too much.

Knowing how to communicate your needs is also important. Be direct, say: 'I feel like shit, I feel like the worst parent, I feel like running away!' If you say how you really feel, you're more likely to get a response which meets your needs. I've yet to meet a friend or professional who thought I was a horrific person for feeling like parenting is overwhelming at times. But we need to normalise these feelings and discuss them more openly. I love my children more than life itself, but autism makes parenting much more challenging and exhausting at times. I am human. You are human. We've got this!

What the experts say

Parenting an autistic child brings unique additional challenges for mothers and fathers.[142] Hartley and Schultz suggest that parents of autistic children often rely on formal supports and services to help them to meet their child's needs, and further carry the burden of unmet need in this context.[142] Karp and Kuo report that maternal mental health is particularly at risk following an autism diagnosis for a child.[143] This is partly related to the worry about waiting times for intervention and what this might mean for their child and family.

Parents' mental health and wellbeing directly impact their parenting ability and capacity to cope with changing circumstances regarding their child's needs.[144] Parents of autistic children are more likely to suffer from depressive disorders and feel more isolated than parents of neurotypical children.[145] Feelings of guilt and not doing enough are common for parents of autistic children.[146] Jellett and colleagues in 2015, found in their study that the challenging behaviour of autistic children can further increase the stress experienced by parents and argue that responding to parents' mental health needs can positively impact on the functioning of the whole family.[147] This highlights the importance for us as parents to remain mindful of our own mental health and do everything we can to promote this. Equally, attending your GP if you feel you may be suffering from a mental health disorder, is an absolute necessity for parents of autistic children. Remember, you need to put your own oxygen mask on first! Some stress, distress and a day here and there of feeling low is okay. But identifying when it's more than this is really important. Depression is so much more than feeling low and can absolutely cripple you as a person. There is help available and you don't have to feel like this.

Below is an outline of some symptoms of depression and stress for parents to be aware of and respond to.

Figure 11.2 Depression and stress symptoms to be aware of

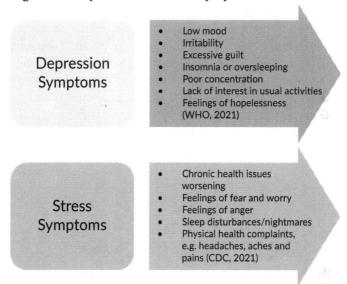

Depression Symptoms
- Low mood
- Irritability
- Excessive guilt
- Insomnia or oversleeping
- Poor concentration
- Lack of interest in usual activities
- Feelings of hopelessness (WHO, 2021)

Stress Symptoms
- Chronic health issues worsening
- Feelings of fear and worry
- Feelings of anger
- Sleep disturbances/nightmares
- Physical health complaints, e.g. headaches, aches and pains (CDC, 2021)

The list above outlines some of the body's reactions to stress and depression. And the expert evidence highlights how common stress and poor mental health are for parents of autistic children. But this doesn't mean that parents should feel this way, or that feeling stressed or unwell are acceptable or par for the course. Education about autism and support groups with other parents of autistic children have been found to reduces stress for parents and increase their coping capacity.

Coping with uncertainty is one of the reasons cited as causing increasing stress and worry for parents of children with autism.[148] This certainly makes sense for me as a parent. Not knowing when meltdowns would occur, or when one of my children would become distressed or overwhelmed meant that I was often worrying thinking of what might happen or what could happen. This can lead to parents avoiding things like events, behaviours or certain situations in an effort to cope with this uncertainty.[148] Parenting support groups have been found to be effective in helping parents to manage their child's behaviour and improve their own coping capacities.[149] Support groups which provide education and an opportunity for parents to discuss their feelings and experiences, can empower parents in supporting their child and reducing challenging behaviours. Providing parents with autism education, enables them to enhance their understanding of autism and to make changes to help their child based on this.[150] The idea is that if a parent knows more about autism, they can use this knowledge to try new methods of behaviour management, to help their child to develop socially or to adapt the environment in order to reduce their child's stress.[150] Farmer and Reupert argue that parents who feel more informed about autism, subsequently feel more confident in their parenting ability and their ability to respond to their child's needs.[151] The additional benefits of attending educational parent support groups further highlight that parents feel less isolated and that they have a better understanding of their child.

KEY LEARNING POINTS FROM THIS CHAPTER:

- That voice in your head is powerful. Tell yourself positive things: 'You are a good parent'; 'Your children will be okay'; 'You are determined'; and 'You can do this!'
- Identify exactly what you need (from friends, family and professionals) and communicate this with them clearly.
- Say no to things that might cause stress for you and your children. It's lovely to catch up with friends and family at events, but if it will cause more stress and upset than enjoyment for your child, sometimes it's best to just say no.
- Prioritise your mental health and wellbeing. You can't pour from an empty cup!
- Create self-care plans for yourself and seek support if you feel you're not coping.
- Know the signs that you might not be coping and be aware of how symptoms of depression or stress may be affecting you.

- Do see your GP if things become overwhelming, and know that there is help and things will get better.
- Find parent support groups or autism educational opportunities. Build your toolkit and feel more empowered in understanding and meeting your child's needs.

Conclusion

This chapter has discussed the emotional challenges of parenting an autistic child and looked at how some parents may feel like they're not coping. My own experiences of this highlight how tough this feeling is to deal with and even to admit to myself and other people. Being aware of how I'm coping and my capacity for parenting is key. Sharing my feelings with others when I feel I'm close to burnout and need support prevents me from reaching breaking point. Finding your 'people' is instrumental to maintaining your own health and wellbeing. We can't be the parent we want to be if we feel overwhelmed or unwell. Mental illness is more common for parents of autistic children. The stresses of parenting a child with additional needs has been well documented within the research. Join support groups, go to an exercise class or go for a coffee with a friend to offload. But if you find yourself really struggling emotionally, please do visit your GP. You will be met with compassion and empathy (in my experience) and not judgement or questioning of your ability to parent, as many of us may fear.

12

A NOTE FOR PROFESSIONALS

Introduction

If sales are good for this book ... it might be due to the multiple professionals who have seen my children over the years buying copies and wondering if they made the cut! However, this book will not drag anyone through the mud. We, as a family, have had the most distressing and gut-wrenching experiences with some professionals, but all of them cared, tried their best, and genuinely wanted to help my children. But equally we have had the most amazing experiences where we left appointments feeling like everything was going to be okay and we weren't on this journey alone. I will give some general examples of both experiences, but will not share the specific profession I'm referring to within my examples, as I must stress that I am forever grateful to each and every professional we have ever interacted with, as every one of them tried to help our family.

This chapter will be addressed to professionals. It will give you my experiences of what went well and what didn't, in the hope that you can use this to guide and inform you in your own practice. This chapter will examine the most effective ways to support parents and families on their autism journey and will discuss what you can do to promote a positive partnership with the parents of the children you are caring for.

My experiences

One of the toughest memories I have regarding interactions with professionals related to Ellie. Ellie was going through a phase of grinding her teeth. We were advised that this was a stim or a tick and to ignore this behaviour. One professional tried to discourage Ellie from doing this and showed her a graphic image of rotting teeth in their efforts to do this. Ellie was hysterical and got such a fright she couldn't catch her breath. She cried and cried and was shaking she was so frightened. I reassured her this would not happen to her teeth and she would be okay. I was so, so angry. Every instinct in my body was raging. I felt I would explode in trying to protect my daughter and felt horrified and shocked that any professional would do something so reckless. I had to really soul search after this experience to find some rationale for why this happened. And again, I do believe in hindsight that this professional thought that this would help to deter the teeth-grinding and help Ellie in the long run. It was a massive mistake on their part however and I vehemently complained. But ... we are all human (I can say this now many years later). We all make mistakes and not one of us is perfect. If you make a mistake as a professional, please own it. Taking responsibility and apologising is usually enough to undo any unintentional harm. And this is vital for a good relationship as you continue to support a family.

Regarding positive experiences, it is tough to choose just one! We have met some of the most amazing and genuine professionals over the years. Some memories still make me smile when I think of them. Alex and Ellie both had to have extensive dental work (extractions, fillings, etc). Alex wasn't diagnosed at the time, but was very unsure about visiting the dentist and what to expect. We didn't know how he would react but we knew he needed to be seen. Alex refused to sit on the chair or open his mouth. He was quite direct in saying no, was stimming and pacing back and forth. I could feel my stress levels rising and was thinking 'This is going to be a disaster'. I was trying to coax him to sit and try at least, but he was not going to do it. Then, out of nowhere, the dentist and dental nurse started being really theatrical... I was a bit taken aback. They were joking and talking to Alex and gently coaxing him. The nurse gave me a wink and I slowly backed out of the room. They had this completely under control. They cajoled Alex and before he knew it he was lying in the chair having his examination. Every time he went to move they distracted him with a funny story or a question, they asked him what nicknames he would give them and who was his favourite. Alex was so distracted and entertained, that before we knew it the dental exam was complete. They were exceptional!

As a family, we have interacted with a broad range of professionals over the years. These include: teachers, SNAs, occupational therapists, physiotherapists, speech and language therapists, social workers, social care workers, psychologists, psychiatrists, clinical nurse managers, play therapists, cognitive behavioural therapists, GPs, public health nurses, paediatricians and Department of Education staff.

Ellie has had the most amazing SNAs over the years. One in particular stands out. She called Ellie 'Ellie Coco Pop'. She absolutely adored her and we still keep in contact. She felt protective towards Ellie, as protective as she would be with her own child. She was so intuitive with Ellie and her needs that she would intervene before a situation escalated. She would create social opportunities for Ellie in school with just one other child (which worked best for Ellie) and she just had her back, completely. The comfort as a mother to know that another person cares so deeply and genuinely for your child in school is indescribable. Years later I learned that this SNA was a special needs mom herself, so she really did understand. And she had a house full of boys and loved spending time with my little girl! I will never forget the care she showed my daughter.

Also, Ellie's school had a club at lunchtime for children who found the yard difficult. The children who were overwhelmed with the hustle and bustle of the busy school yard, or those who found themselves getting into scuffles or disagreements more frequently, were invited (by choice) to attend the lunchtime club a couple of days a week. They were supported in small groups to play board games, build their social skills and generally develop without the pressure of the school yard. In hindsight this was quite innovative ten years ago and a really proactive and inclusive initiative by the school.

Another moment that really stands out was when we had been trying for over a year to teach Alex to ride a bike. He just couldn't get the hang of it with his dyspraxia and he was starting to feel self-conscious riding his bike with stabilisers. Alex's provider regularly sent forms asking what he needed help with. So we got a letter in the post about a learn-to-cycle camp over Easter break. We dropped Alex off at 11.00 a.m. When we picked him up at 1.30 p.m. he was cycling with no stabilisers! I burst into tears; I couldn't believe it. They had initially taken off the pedals to help him to balance. We were so overwhelmed and proud that we bought Alex a brand new bike on the way home!

We, as a family, will remember what you, as a professional, did on all of these wonderful occasions. We will know you helped our child in way that we couldn't. We will know that without your help our children may not have reached for the stars as they should! But please also know that relying on other people to help us as we parent our children can be a tough pill to swallow initially. We all imagine parenting and doing so well without help. We hope we are enough for our children and can meet all of their needs. So acknowledging and adjusting to having you help us with our most important task in the world (parenting) can take time.

What do parents need when they meet with professionals?

We need you to listen, *really* listen. I remember having lists of Ellie's behaviours when we got to appointments. It sounds bizarre, right? But when your child is biting you, really hurting their sibling and doing dangerous things all the time, you feel like you need to do something, anything to help them and keep them safe. I didn't know what else to do. I responded to each crisis as it arose and did my best to prevent them from happening. But I didn't really know how to help my own child. This is a really horrible feeling for a parent. I felt like I was failing. So making a list of each incident, its frequency and severity, made me feel like I was doing something which might shed light on the cause of these behaviours and what we could do to help. I felt desperate, desperate to help my child, desperate to understand why she was having behavioural, sensory and emotional issues. I thought that by sharing my lists with professionals, a lightbulb moment would happen and someone would say:

'Ahh, I know exactly what's causing this.' And then we would know exactly how to help. So what may have been perceived as me being strange, overly focused on the negatives, or even obsessive, was in fact me being absolutely desperate to help my child.

When your child seriously hurts their cousin or a neighbour's child, you desperately want to be able to explain this behaviour and address it. As much for your child as anyone else's. To see your child labelled as the bold one, the strange one, the naughty one who no one wants to play with is hard to bear. Having an explanation or diagnosis presents hope.

You have a lot of responsibility as a professional, every word you say may be etched in the minds of these parents and their child forever. Your impact within your interactions with families of children with autism or suspected autism (or displaying challenging behaviour), can make or break a parent who might be on the edge. Some parents you meet may not have shared their concerns or worries about their child with anyone else, you may be the first person they have spoken to about this.

Teachers, you may be the person who has to broach this subject with a parent who perhaps has no idea that their child may be autistic. This is far beyond your training and your pay grade, but it's a situation many teachers find themselves in. Take your time to plan your words carefully. Be very gentle in your approach and do highlight the child's amazing qualities, in addition to their difficulties. Ensure you have an appropriate space when speaking to parents at school. At the classroom door, when lots of children and parents are coming and going, isn't always appropriate. Make an appointment with them or book another room so you can speak privately.

I think my experiences, both positive and negative, have given me a unique insight into what works, what doesn't and what best practice should look like. What I've learned from my journey is that to help parents of children presenting with autism, ADHD or any behavioural or emotional issues, you must support the parents. When I felt I wasn't listened to, or that professionals thought my child's needs were exaggerated or perhaps not as serious as I thought they were, this really negatively affected me emotionally. When I'm not feeling well emotionally or mentally, this impacts my ability to cope with my child's needs. For example, after a stressful appointment, if my child's needs are minimised, or if I feel judged, when I leave I'm upset. If Alex has a meltdown in the car on the way home, I will react with stress, my patience is thin and I can feel the tension and stress in our interactions increasing. The minute I'm stressed, the kids act up more. And the negative cycle of interaction is initiated.

However, if I attend an appointment and feel listened to, understood, and that my child's needs are recognised (even if no intervention or plan is offered), I leave feeling like I can cope, like I am believed, like I have a professional who gets it and is willing to try to help. Then I go home feeling relief, feeling hopeful and that 'I can do this'. This enables me to cope with whatever that day or week might bring up for my children. So a positive feedback loop has been created where my reactions are positive to my children even in very challenging situations, I'm coping better and don't feel so alone on my journey.

Open your toolbox

I had a moment which really stands out a few years later when I was sitting a class while studying for my Masters in Social Work. It was quite early on in our autism journey and we were learning in college about a solution-focused approach. As soon as it was explained.... I could see our own interventions as a family in a completely different light. Everything slowly fell into place. I remember leaving sessions with my children so upset, as I felt my concerns weren't listened to by professionals, or that professionals didn't understand the gravity of some of the safety issues we were facing in trying to manage our child's behaviour and protect our other children. I couldn't understand why the professionals were consistently deflecting from the issues we as a family were struggling with and coming to them for help with.

A solution-focused approach (I found out) looks for the positive, asks when did the behaviour *not* occur, questions how you resolved the issue, etc? It asks how can we support you to do this again? A solution-focused approach does not dwell on or explore the problem (behaviour), but instead focuses on solutions.[152] But when I went to our appointments, I was desperate to discuss these challenges that were making our family life so difficult. I was desperate to feel heard and help my child. I didn't understand at that time that the professionals were trying to help us using a solution-focused approach.

Had I known this at the time, and had I understood this approach, it would have reduced the confusion I felt about some professionals' responses to our family's needs. It would have reduced the upset I felt at not being listened to or heard, and it would have alleviated the feeling that really challenging issues and problems were being ignored.

As a professional, sharing with families the approach you are using is beneficial in two ways:

1. Families understand why you are responding as you are, what is expected of them, and what you hope the outcome will be. This way expectations are clear from the outset. And if either party feels the approach is not working or needs modifying, they can raise this. This will result in a clearer more transparent plan of action for the family, and everyone being on the same page about the approach. It will reduce misunderstandings in communication and will increase the likelihood of a more successful outcome. While this sharing of information further signifies a partnership approach with parents and fosters positive relationships with professionals.

2. Sharing information with families about the approach you are taking, or a theory you are basing your response to their needs upon, is providing them with the knowledge and education to hopefully help themselves with this insight going forward. For example, supporting a family based on Bowen's Family Systems theory[153] might mean supporting a dad to address addiction issues, or sourcing childcare resources for a single mom struggling with no family support. However, when families don't know the rationale for this, they may feel that their behaviour or circumstances are being blamed for their child's needs or behaviours. Whereas understanding the impact of each family member's wellbeing on others may help parents to become more aware of the significance of self-care and addressing their own health needs, and so on. Building the family's toolkit

to help themselves and their children going forward should be a key element of any support plan for an autistic child.

Relationships between parents and professionals

For me, the relationships I have with the professionals who support my children and my family, are the strongest indicators for a positive experience and a subsequent positive outcome. If we have an appointment and things have been particularly difficult in the lead-up to this, the response of the professional I meet is even more powerful. Even if you can't offer answers, or can't offer additional supports, how you speak, how you listen and how you communicate with the parent will have an impact on them and their family long after they leave your appointment. Having a positive relationship with parents, directly impacts the outcome for their child. Parental capacity and coping is more likely if they feel you are an ally and on their side.

When I attend an appointment where the professional I meet makes an effort to build rapport with me, to speak to my child, to ask how we 'really' are, I leave this appointment feeling lighter. Nothing might have changed, no additional supports or interventions may have been offered, but having a positive meeting with someone who cares and really 'gets' it, means I leave feeling better. When I'm feeling better, my parenting is better, my response to my children's needs is more positive, and a cycle of positive interaction within my family is set in motion.

Conversely, when I meet a professional with poor communication skills, who is preoccupied or appears to have no desire to do anything other than get us out the door, I leave feeling defeated, deflated and worse than when I arrived. I'm then upset in my parenting, less patient, more overwhelmed and less capable of meeting my child's needs in the best possible way.

Your role as a professional is so powerful. It's a massive amount of responsibility, but can be truly transformative for families and can profoundly positively impact their lives. Carl Rogers a psychotherapist proposed in 1951 that three core conditions are necessary within a helping relationship to promote therapeutic change: empathy, congruence or genuineness and unconditional positive regard. Empathy is about truly envisioning another person's perspective and trying to see the world through their eyes. Congruence or genuineness is concerned with you as the professional being yourself and being authentic in your interactions with parents and families. And finally, unconditional positive regard is about the professional accepting and valuing the person they are helping, without judgement.[154] Wickman and Campbell[155] argue that Carl Rogers' core conditions have proven so effective, that they are still considered essential components of helping relationships today.

Bradford suggests that parents and families largely need information from professionals as they navigate their child's autism journey. Parents benefit from educational resources to help them to learn more about autism and how best to support their child. While information provision further helps parents to feel more empowered as they adjust to their child's diagnosis.[156]

Parents' experiences of interacting with professionals during autism assessments and therapies have also been examined in previous research. Boshoff and colleagues[157] reported that some parents had their concerns for their child dismissed, or were told that their child's behaviour and presentation during an appointment was viewed as 'normal' and their children presented as not having any additional needs. I can tell you, this is beyond frustrating. In our case, we would feel like we were living in a hurricane right up until we walked in to the appointment, and then Ellie would be angelic: no biting, screaming, raging, just calmness. We wouldn't even make it to the car after the appointment before the challenging behaviour would start happening again. An appointment with a professional is such a minute part of a child's life. Being in a different environment, usually without siblings and often where lots of new toys and art supplies are available, meant that often, behaviours of concern were not visible. But as time progressed, it was impossible for Ellie to maintain a calm demeanour. And equally to note, as understanding of autism is developing, professionals are more aware of the subtle signs of communication difficulties and sensory distress.

But, as professionals, more than anything, please be super careful with the words you use. If a parent feels close to not coping, is fighting against the tide to find out how to help their child and is feeling overwhelmed, saying he/she looks perfectly fine isn't helpful. Try to be mindful when communicating with parents who are likely desperate for help, that the clinic setting and in such a short space of time, usually isn't a sufficient snapshot from which to come to firm conclusions without further in-depth assessment.

Working in partnership with parents is a fundamental prerequisite for successful helping relationships, when supporting an autistic child and their family. According to Brookman-Frazee and Koegel,[158] partnership working consists of agreed actions and outcomes between professionals and parents, where both parties take ownership and responsibility. In fact, when compared to clinician-/professional-led interventions based in one particular study, partnership approaches were more successful in producing positive outcomes for children and parents.[158] Vlcek and colleagues in their study found that partnership working between parents, teachers and healthcare providers, resulted in consistency for children across settings,[159] So if the child's goal is agreed, all parties involved can offer appropriate supports in school, at home and at health service appointments/therapies, to help the child to reach their goals. Such an agreement further levels the playing field between each person responsible for helping the child, with each bringing their own unique insight on the child's needs in each setting and consequently enabling an informed and comprehensive plan for care.

Goldman and Burke[160] suggest that home-school communication is of further significance for autistic children. The communication difficulties which come with autism mean that communication from teachers, special needs assistants or resource staff may be needed more frequently to ensure the child has their educational needs met. For example, with Alex, his SNA will text me if ingredients are needed for cooking, or if events are coming up where Alex needs to change his routine, or bring additional items for school. This small act is so helpful. It means I can remind and prepare Alex for the change and ensure he has everything he needs. The alternative may be that Alex forgets what he needs, or that if a change of event is coming up and he is unprepared for it, it could become really distressing for him as a result.

Whitaker reports that what parents need most from professionals is to be equipped with the tools to support their child themselves.[161]

The sheer volume and breadth of information online about autism can be daunting for parents of newly diagnosed children. Signposting to useful information and resources is helpful in addition to helping parents better understand their child's needs, and how to identify and respond to these.[161] Elder and D'Alessandro propose that parents often need direction from professionals about what to do next after receiving an autism diagnosis for their child.[162] Answering questions will form a substantial part of interactions with parents in the initial aftermath of a diagnosis, and this is a central element of the professional's role at this time.

Engaging in continuing professional development (CPD) is a further pertinent responsibility of professionals supporting autistic children and families. CPD occurs when a practitioner intentionally engages in training, research or development, after their initial qualification.[163] CPD is described as a continual process of knowledge acquisition and skills development which acknowledges the evolution of knowledge and understanding surrounding the area of practice.[163] CPD can enhance the competency of the professional and enhance the care provision for the child and their family.[164] While collaboration between professionals is another effective method of knowledge generation and professionals can further contribute to the growing body of research surrounding autism themselves.[165]

In summary, professionals have a particularly substantial role in supporting parents and families of autistic children. This role is even more significant at the time of, or immediately after, an autism diagnosis. Parents will feel overwhelmed with the volume of information available, so should be directed to the most accurate and relevant sources of education as they begin their journey of supporting their autistic child. Equally, your role as a professional at this very sensitive time is momentous. Confused, worried and upset parents are looking to you for answers to help and guide them through what is their new reality. Therefore, a gentle, kind and non-judgemental approach is essential.

> ### KEY LEARNING POINTS FROM THIS CHAPTER:
>
> - Professionals have a central and significant role in supporting autistic children and their families.
> - Families might be stressed, worried about the future and struggling to cope emotionally when they meet you in your school/office/clinic.
> - Parents will remember every single word you say (particularly when confirming a diagnosis of autism), so plan your approach carefully.
> - Feeling listened to and heard can result in families leaving appointments feeling more positive and relieved.
> - Working in partnership with parents is a beneficial strategy for all involved and maximises positive outcomes for children.
> - Share strategies, theories, approaches and ideas.
> - Remain empathetic, genuine and non-judgemental.[154]

Conclusion

This chapter described some of my own experiences with my family and our interactions with professionals. Reflecting on these interactions, and having gained life and parental experience, I hope enables me to provide you with a unique insight regarding helpful and not-so-helpful practices, when supporting autistic children and their families. Substantial responsibility (and likely pressure!) comes with your role and therefore thoughtful, individually tailored and helpful information and care provision, are fundamental to promote the effectiveness of your interactions. Sharing your insight and approaches with families can act as an empowering mechanism for supporting parents to support their children. Working in partnership with parents and providing information and educational resources, are further necessary elements of successful interventions to support autistic children. Finally, upskilling and engaging in regular continued professional development will ensure you are delivering supports based on best practice and the most up-to-date evidence, which will maximise the success of outcomes for the families you provide care to.

FULL REFERENCE LIST

1. Christensen DL, Braun KVN, Baio J, et al. Prevalence and characteristics of Autism Spectrum Disorder among children aged 8 years – Autism and Developmental Disabilities Monitoring Network, 11 Sites, United States, 2012. *Morbidity and Mortality Weekly Report Surveillance Summaries* (Washington DC, 2002) 2018; 65(13) doi: 10.15585/mmwr.ss6513a1

2. Silverman C. *Understanding Autism: Parents, Doctors, and the History of a Disorder.* Princeton: Princeton University Press; 2011.

3. World Health Organization. Autism spectrum disorders, Geneva: WHO; 2021 [internet]. Available from: https://www.who.int/news-room/fact-sheets/detail/autism-spectrum-disorders

4. Asperger H. Die „Autistischen Psychopathen" im Kindesalter. *Archiv für Psychiatrie und Nervenkrankheiten* 1944;117(1):76–136. doi:10.1007/BF01837709

5. Woodbury-Smith MR, Volkmar FR. Asperger syndrome. *European Child & Adolescent Psychiatry* 2009;18(1) doi: 10.1007/s00787-008-0701-0

6. Falk D, Schofield E. *Geeks, Genes and the Evolution of Asperger Syndrome*, University of New Mexico Press; 2018.

7. American Psychiatric Association. *Diagnostic and Statistic Manual of Mental Disorders.* Arlington: American Psychiatric Publishing; 5th ed, 2013.

8. Ghaziuddin M, Ghaziuddin N, Greden J. Depression in persons with autism: implications for research and clinical care. *Journal of Autism and Developmental Disorders* 2002;32(4) doi: 10.1023/a:1016330802348

9. Ortiz J. *The Myriad Gifts of Asperger's Syndrome.* London: Jessica Kingsley; 2008.

10. Huang JP, Cui SS, Han Y, et al. Prevalence and early signs of autism spectrum disorder (ASD) among 18–36 month-old children of Tianjin in China. *Biomedical and Environmental Sciences: BES* 2014;27(6) doi: 10.3967/bes2014.008

11. Sicherman N, Charite J, Eyal G, et al. Clinical signs associated with earlier diagnosis of children with autism spectrum disorder. *Biomedical Central Pediatrics* 2021;21(1) doi: 10.1186/s12887-021-02551-0

12. McPheeters ML, Weitlauf A, Vehorn A, et al. Screening for Autism Spectrum Disorder in young children: a systematic evidence review for the U.S. Preventive Services Task Force. *Agency for Healthcare Research and Quality Publications* 2016;13(129):202.

13. Yirmiya N, Charman T. The prodrome of autism: early behavioral and biological signs, regression, peri- and post-natal development and genetics. *Journal of Child Psychology and Psychiatry, and Allied disciplines* 2010;51(4) doi:10.1111/j.1469-7610.2010.02214.x

14. CDC. Autism spectrum disorder ASD. 2021 [internet: updated 2021-03-29T01:52:34Z.] Available from: https://www.cdc.gov/ncbddd/autism/signs.html

15. American Psychiatric Association. *Diagnostic and Statistical Manual of Mental Disorders*. American Psychiatric Publishing; 4th ed, 1994.

16. HSE. Assessing your child's disability 2021 [internet]. Available from: https://www.hse.ie/eng/services/list/4/disability/disability-assessment/.

17. Hull L, Petrides KV, Allison C, et al. 'Putting on my best normal': social camouflaging in adults with autism spectrum conditions. *Journal of Autism and Developmental Disorders* 2017;47(8) doi: 10.1007/s10803-017-3166-5

18. Cage E, Troxell-Whitman Z. Understanding the reasons, contexts and costs of camouflaging for autistic adults. *Journal of Autism and Developmental Disorders* 2019;49(5) doi: 10.1007/s10803-018-03878-x

19. Pearson A, Rose K. A conceptual analysis of autistic masking: understanding the narrative of stigma and the illusion of choice. *Autism in Adulthood* 2021;3(1) doi: 10.1089/aut.2020.0043

20. Irish Society for Autism. Assessment and diagnosis 2021 [internet]. Available from: https://autism.ie/information/faq/assessment-and-diagnosis/.

21. Thabtah F, Peebles D. Early autism screening: a comprehensive review. *International Journal of Environmental Reseach in Public Health* 2019;16(18) doi: 10.3390/ijerph16183502

22. American Psychiatric Association. *Diagnostic and Statistic Manual of Mental Disorders*. Arlington: American Psychiatric Publishing; 5th ed, 2013.

23. Kulage KM, Smaldone AM, Cohn EG. How will DSM-5 affect autism diagnosis? A systematic literature review and meta-analysis. *Journal of Autism and Developmental Disorders* 2014;44(8) doi: 10.1007/s10803-014-2065-2

24. CDC. Diagnostic criteria | Autism Spectrum Disorder (ASD): Centre for Disease Control and Prevention; 2020 [internet: updated 2020-06-29T06:28:06Z]. Available from: https://www.cdc.gov/ncbddd/autism/hcp-dsm.html

25. Lynch T. The validity of the DSM: An overview. *Practitioner Perspective* 2018;18(2):5–10.

26. Rosenberg R. Abnormal is the new normal: Why will half of the U.S. population have a diagnosable mental disorder? *Slate, Health and Science*, 2013.

27. Akshoomoff N, Corsello C, Schmidt H. The role of the autism diagnostic observation schedule in the assessment of Autism Spectrum Disorders in school and community settings. *The California School Psychologist: CASP* 2006;11 doi: 10.1007/BF03341111

28. Le Couteur AL, Lord C, Rutter, M. *The Autism Diagnostic Interview-Revised (ADI-R)*. Los Angeles: Western Psychological Services, 2003.

29. Crane L, Chester JW, Goddard L, et al. Experiences of autism diagnosis: A survey of over 1,000 parents in the United Kingdom. *Autism: the International Journal of Research and Practice* 2016;20(2) doi: 10.1177/1362361315573636

30. Mansell W, Morris K. A survey of parents' reactions to the diagnosis of an autistic spectrum disorder by a local service: access to information and use of services. *Autism: the International Journal of Research and Practice* 2004;8(4) doi: 10.1177/1362361304045213

31. Ozonoff S, Young GS, Steinfeld MB, et al. How early do parent concerns predict later autism diagnosis? *Journal of Developmental and Behavioral Pediatrics: JDBP* 2009;30(5) doi: 10.1097/dbp.0b013e3181ba0fcf

32. Rhoades RA, Scarpa A, Salley B. The importance of physician knowledge of autism spectrum disorder: results of a parent survey. *Biomedical Central Pediatrics* 2007;7 doi: 10.1186/1471-2431-7-37

33. Hayes J, Ford T, McCabe R, et al. Autism diagnosis as a social process. *Autism: the International Journal of Research and Practice* 2021 doi: 10.1177/13623613211030392

34. HSE. Tell me about the PDS programme. 2021 [internet]. Available from: https://www.hse.ie/eng/services/list/4/disability/progressing-disability/pds-programme/

35. Abbott M, Bernard P, Forge J. Communicating a diagnosis of Autism Spectrum Disorder – a qualitative study of parents' experiences. *Clinical Child Psychology and Psychiatry* 2013;18(3) doi: 10.1177/1359104512455813

36. Rasmussen PS, Pedersen IK, Pagsberg AK. Biographical disruption or cohesion?: How parents deal with their child's autism diagnosis. *Social Science and Medicine* 2020;244(244):112673. doi: 10.1016/j.socscimed.2019.112673

37. Anderberg E, South M. Predicting parent reactions at diagnostic disclosure sessions for autism. *Journal of Autism and Developmental Disorders* 2021;51(10) doi: 10.1007/s10803-020-04817-5

38. Gentles SJ, Nicholas DB, Jack SM, et al. Coming to understand the child has autism: A process illustrating parents' evolving readiness for engaging in care. *Autism* 2020;24(2):470–83. doi: 10.1177_1362361319874647

39. Banach M, Iudice J, Conway L, et al. Family Support and Empowerment: Post Autism Diagnosis Support Group for Parents. *Social Work with Groups* 2010;33(1):69–83. doi: http://dx.doi.org/10.1080/01609510903437383

40. Jacobs D, Steyaert J, Dierickx K, et al. Parents' multi-layered expectations when requesting an Autism Spectrum Disorder assessment of their young child: an in-depth interview study. *Biomedical Central Psychiatry* 2020;20(1):440. doi: 10.1186/s12888-020-02806-7

41. Courcy I, des Rivières-Pigeon C. 'We're responsible for the diagnosis and for finding help'. The help-seeking trajectories of families of children on the autism spectrum. *Sociology of Health & Illness* 2021;43(1) doi: 10.1111/1467-9566.13184

42. Lopez K, Magana S, Xu Y, et al. Mother's reaction to autism diagnosis: A qualitative analysis comparing Latino and White parents. *Journal of Rehabilitation* 2018;84(1):41–50. doi: http://dx.doi.org/

43. Kuhn JC, Carter AS. Maternal self-efficacy and associated parenting cognitions among mothers of children with autism. *The American Journal of Orthopsychiatry* 2006;76(4):564–75. doi: 10.1037/0002-9432.76.4.564

44. Potter CA. 'I received a leaflet and that is all': Father experiences of a diagnosis of autism. *British Journal of Learning Disabilities* 2017;45(2):95–105. doi: 10.1111/bld.12179

45. Poslawsky IE, Naber FB, Van Daalen E, et al. Parental reaction to early diagnosis of their children's autism spectrum disorder: an exploratory study. *Child Psychiatry and Human Development* 2014;45(3):294–305. doi: 10.1007/s10578-013-0400-z

46. Da Paz NS, Siegel B, Coccia MA, et al. Acceptance or despair? Maternal adjustment to having a child diagnosed with autism. *Journal of Autism and Developmental Disorders* 2018;48(6) doi: 10.1007/s10803-017-3450-4

47. Murphy T & Tierney K. Parents of children with autistic spectrum disorders (ASD): A survey of information needs. Report to the National Council for Special Education Special Education Research Initiative, 2014.

48. Bravo-Benítez J, Pérez-Marfil MN, Román-Alegre B, et al. Grief experiences in family caregivers of children with Autism Spectrum Disorder (ASD). *International Journal of Environmental Research Public Health* 2019;16(23):4821. doi: 10.3390/ijerph16234821

49. O'Brien B. Ambiguous loss in families of children with Autism Spectrum Disorders*. *Family Relations* 2007;56(2):135–46. doi: 10.1111/j.1741-3729.2007.00447.x

50. Boss P. *Ambiguous Loss: Learning to Live with Unresolved Grief.* Harvard University Press; 1999.

51. Bujnowska AM, Rodríguez C, García T, et al. Parenting and future anxiety: the impact of having a child with developmental disabilities. *International Journal of Environmental Research Public Health* 2019;16(4) doi: 10.3390/ijerph16040668

52. McCabe H. The importance of parent-to-parent support among families of children with autism in the People's Republic of China. *International Journal of Disability, Development & Education* 2008;55(4):303–14. doi: International Journal of Disability, Development and Education, Vol. 55, No. 4, December 2008, pp 303–314.

53. Shepherd D, Goedeke S, Landon J, et al. The types and functions of social supports used by parents caring for a child with Autism Spectrum Disorder. *Journal of Autism and Developmental Disorders* 2020;50(4):1337–52. doi: 10.1007/s10803-019-04359-5

54. Crane L, Jones L, Prosser R, et al. Parents' views and experiences of talking about autism with their children. *Autism: the International Journal of Research and Practice* 2019;23(8):1969–81. doi: 10.1177/1362361319836257

55. Pike R. Talking together about an Autism diagnosis. A guide for parents and carers of children with an autism spectrum disorder. National Autistic Society. 2008 [internet]. Available from: https://www.autism.org.uk/shop/products/books-and-resources/autism-talking-about-a-diagnosis

56. American Academy of Paediatrics. Discussing the diagnosis of autism spectrum disorder with your child. 2021 [internet] Available from: https://publications.aap.org/patiented/pages/c_ASD_handouts

57. CAR. Telling your child about an ASD diagnosis. 2020 [internet]. Available from: https://www.carautismroadmap.org/telling-your-child-about-an-asd-diagnosis/

58. Dundon R. *Talking with Your Child about Their Autism Diagnosis: A Guide for Parents.* London: Jessica Kingsley Publishers; 2018.

59. Finnegan R, Trimble T, Egan J. Irish parents' lived experience of learning about and adapting to their child's autistic spectrum disorder diagnosis and their process of telling their child about their diagnosis. *Irish Journal of Psychology* 2014;35(2–3):78–90. doi: 10.1080/03033910.2014.982143

60. Jones G. Giving the diagnosis to the young person with Asperger Syndrome or high functioning autism. *Good Autism Practice* 2001;2(2):65–73.

61. Huws JC, Jones RS. Diagnosis, disclosure, and having autism: an interpretative phenomenological analysis of the perceptions of young people with autism. *Journal of Intellectual & Developmental Disability* 2008;33(2):99–107. doi: 10.1080/13668250802010394

62. Wheeler M. Getting started: Introducing your child to his/her diagnosis of autism. Bloomington: Indiana University; 2020 [internet]. Available from: https://www.iidc.indiana.edu/irca/learn-about-autism/getting-started-introducing-your-child-to-his-or-her-diagnosis-of-autism.html.

63. Foden T. ASD diagnosis. What do we tell the kids? Interactive Autism Network. 2010 [internet]. Available from: https://iancommunity.org/cs/articles/telling_a_child_about_his_asd

64. Lodder A, Papadopoulos C, Randhawa G. Stigma of living as an autism carer: a brief psycho-social support intervention (SOLACE). Study protocol for a randomised controlled feasibility study. *Pilot and Feasibility Studies* 2019;5(1):1–8. doi: doi:10.1186/s40814-019-0406-9

65. Neely-Barnes SL, Hall HR, Roberts RJ, et al. Parenting a child with an Autism Spectrum Disorder: public perceptions and parental conceptualizations. *Journal of Family Social Work* 2011;14(3):208–25. doi: Journal of Family Social Work, 14, (3) May–June, 2011: pp 208–225.

66. Myers BJ, Mackintosh, VH, & Goin-Kochel, RP. 'My greatest joy and my greatest heart ache:' Parents' own words on how having a child in the autism spectrum has affected their lives and their families' lives. *Research in Autism Spectrum Disorders* 2009;3(3):670–84. doi: http://dx.doi.org/10.1016/j.rasd.2009.01.004

67. Gray DE. 'Everybody just freezes. Everybody is just embarrassed': felt and enacted stigma among parents of children with high functioning autism. *Sociology of Health & Illness* 2002;24(6):734–49. doi: 10.1111/1467-9566.00316

68. Kinnear SH, Link BG, Ballan MS, et al. Understanding the experience of stigma for parents of children with Autism Spectrum Disorder and the role stigma plays in families' lives. *Journal of Autism and Developmental Disorders* 2016;46(3):942–53. doi: 10.1007/s10803-015-2637-9

69. Ling CYM, Mak, WWS & Cheng, JNS. Attribution model of stigma towards children with autism in Hong Kong. *Journal of Applied Research in Intellectual Disabilities* 2010;23:237–49. doi: 10.1111/j.1468-3148.2008.00456.x

70. Quinn DM, Earnshaw VA. Concealable stigmatized identities and psychological well-being. *Social and Personality Psychology Compass* 2013;7(1):40–51. doi: 10.1111/spc3.12005

71. Alshaigi K, Albraheem R, Alsaleem K, et al. Stigmatization among parents of autism spectrum disorder children in Riyadh, Saudi Arabia. *International Journal of Pediatrics & Adolescent Medicine* 2020;7(3):140–46. doi: 10.1016/j.ijpam.2019.06.003

72. Chiang HM. Expressive communication of children with autism: the use of challenging behaviour. *Journal of Intellectual Disability Research: JIDR* 2008;52(11):966–72. doi: 10.1111/j.1365-2788.2008.01042.x

73. Bedrossian L. Understand autism meltdowns and share strategies to minimize, manage occurrences. *Disability Compliance for Higher Education* 2015;20(7):6. doi: 10.1002/dhe.30026

74. Mazefsky CA. Managing problem emotions and behaviors in children with ASD: an assessment-driven three-step approach. *Language Learning and Education* 2012;19(2):38–47. doi: 1940774200190002038

75. James DM, Fisher S, Vincent S. Challenging behaviour around challenging behaviour. *Journal of Applied Research in Intellectual Disabilities: JARID* 2021;34(4):1166–79. doi: 10.1111/jar.12879

76. Bronfenbrenner U. *The Ecology of Human Development: Experiments by Nature and Design.* Cambridge, Massachusetts: Harvard University Press; 1979.

77. Mugno D, Ruta L, D'Arrigo VG, et al. Impairment of quality of life in parents of children and adolescents with pervasive developmental disorder. *Health and Quality of Life Outcomes* 2007;5(22) doi: 10.1186/1477-7525-5-22

78. Montaque I, Dallos R, McKenzie B. 'It feels like something difficult is coming back to haunt me': An exploration of 'meltdowns' associated with autistic spectrum disorder from a parental perspective. *Clinical Child Psychology and Psychiatry* 2018;23(1):125–39. doi: 10.1177/1359104517730114

79. Moyes R. *Addressing the Challenging Behavior of Children with High-functioning Autism/Asperger Syndrome in the Classroom: A Guide for Teachers and Parents.* London: Jessica Kingsley; 2002.

80. Lewis P. *Achieving Best Behavior for Children with Developmental Disabilities: A Step-by-step Workbook for Parents and Carers.* Philadelphia: Jessica Kingsley; 2006.

81. Morawska, A., & Sanders, M. (2011). Parental use of time out revisited: A useful or harmful parenting strategy? *Journal of Child and Family Studies*, 20. 1-8. http://dx.doi.org.pacificlib.idm.oclc.org/10.1007/s10826-010-9371-x

82. Corralejo, S., Jensen, S., & Greathouse, D. (2018) Time-out for sibling aggression: An analysis of effective durations in a natural setting, *Child & Family Behavior Therapy*, 40:3, 187-203, DOI: 10.1080/07317107.2018.1487701

83. Lantieri, L. (2008). Building inner resilience. *Reclaiming Children and Youth*, 17(2), 43-46.

84. Housman, D.K. (2017). The importance of emotional competence and self-regulation from birth: a case for the evidence-based emotional cognitive social early learning approach. *International Journal of Childcare and Education Policy* 11, 13. https://doi.org/10.1186/s40723-017-0038-6

85. Coogan D. *Child to Parent Violence and Abuse. Family Interventions with Non-Violent Resistance*. London: Jessica Kingsley; 2018.

86. Schorr-Sapir I, Gershy N, Apter A, et al. Parent training in non-violent resistance for children with attention deficit hyperactivity disorder: a controlled outcome study. *European Child & Adolescent Psychiatry* 2021 doi: 10.1007/s00787-021-01723-8

87. Omer H, Lebowitz ER. Nonviolent resistance: helping caregivers reduce problematic behaviors in children and adolescents. *Journal of Marital and Family Therapy* 2016;42(4):688–700. doi: 10.1111/jmft.12168

88. Oxleas NHS Foundation Trust. Guidelines for parents of children or adolescents with violent or destructive behaviours. An eye for an eye will make the whole world blind. 2007 [internet]. Available from: http://oxleas.nhs.uk/site-media/cms-downloads/NVR_for_parents_web_mgRKEiw.pdf

89. Rodda A, Estes A. Beyond social skills: supporting peer relationships and friendships for school-aged children with Autism Spectrum Disorder. *Seminars in Speech and Language* 2018;39(2):178–94. doi: 10.1055/s-0038-1628369

90. Green J, Gilchrist A, Burton D, et al. Social and psychiatric functioning in adolescents with Asperger syndrome compared with conduct disorder. *Journal of Autism and Developmental Disorders* 2000;30(4):279–93. doi: 10.1023/a:1005523232106

91. Bauminger N, Solomon M, Aviezer A, et al. Children with autism and their friends: a multidimensional study of friendship in high-functioning autism spectrum disorder. *Journal of Abnormal Child Psychology* 2008;36(2):135–50. doi: 10.1007/s10802-007-9156-x

92. Chang YC, Shih W, Kasari C. Friendships in preschool children with Autism Spectrum Disorder: What holds them back, child characteristics or teacher behavior? *Autism: the International Journal of Research and Practice* 2016;20(1):65–74. doi: 10.1177/1362361314567761

93. Boutot EA, Bryant, DP. Social integration of students with autism in mainstream settings. *Education and Training in Developmental Disabilities* 2005;40(1):14–23.

94. Bauminger N, Kasari C. Loneliness and friendship in high-functioning children with autism. *Child Development* 2000;71(2):447–56. doi: 10.1111/1467-8624.00156

95. Berkovits LD, Moody CT, Blacher J. 'I don't feel different. But then again, I wouldn't know what it feels like to be normal': perspectives of adolescents with Autism Spectrum Disorder. *Journal of Autism and Developmental Disorders* 2020;50(3):831–43. doi: 10.1007/s10803-019-04309-1

96. Cridland EK, Jones SC, Caputi P, et al. Being a girl in a boys' world: investigating the experiences of girls with autism spectrum disorders during adolescence. *Journal of Autism and Developmental Disorders* 2014;44(6):1261–74. doi: 10.1007/s10803-013-1985-6

97. IACST. What is craniosacral therapy? 2021 [internet]. Available from: https://iacst.ie/craniosacral-therapy

98. Taylor L. Is bio energy therapy a viable resource within the counselling setting? *Éisteach:* Irish Association for Counselling and Psychotherapy, 2016, 16(1).

99. LeClerc S, Easley D. Pharmacological therapies for autism spectrum disorder: a review. *P & T: A Peer-reviewed Journal for Formulary Management* 2015;40(6):389–97.

100. Gupta M, Hoover G. Lurasidone: an effective alternative for the treatment of irritability associated with Autism Spectrum Disorder. *Cureus* 2020;12(12):e12360. doi: 10.7759/cureus.12360

101. Hirsch LE, Pringsheim T. Aripiprazole for autism spectrum disorders (ASD). *The Cochrane Database of Systematic Reviews* 2016;2016(6) doi: 10.1002/14651858. CD009043.pub3

102. Lucchelli JP, Bertschy G. Low-dose Fluoxetine in four children with Autistic Spectrum Disorder improves self-injurious behavior, ADHD-like symptoms, and irritability. *Case Reports in Psychiatry* 2018;2018 doi: 10.1155/2018/6278501

103. Rast JA K, Roux A, Shattuck P. Medication use in youth with autism and Attention-Deficit/Hyperactivity Disorder. *Academic Pediatrics* 2021;21(2):272–79. doi: http://dx.doi.org/10.1016/j.acap.2020.05.015

104. Santosh PS, J. Drug treatment of autism spectrum disorder and its comorbidities in children and adolescents. *British Journal of Psychiatric Advances* 2016;22(3):151–61. doi: doi:10.1192/apt.bp.115.014597

105. Brent S. *Medicating Children: A Guide to Psychiatric Services in Schools.* London: Routledge; 2012.

106. Sparks JA, Duncan BL. The ethics and science of medicating children. *Ethical Human Psychology and Psychiatry* 2004;6(1):25–39.

107. Isaacs D. Attention-deficit/hyperactivity disorder: are we medicating for social disadvantage? *Journal of Paediatrics and Child Health* 2006;42(9):544–47. doi: 10.1111/j.1440-1754.2006.00919.x

108. Mayes RE J, Bagwell C. Medicating children: the enduring controversy over ADHD and pediatric stimulant pharmacotherapy. *Child and Adolescent Psychopharmacology News* 2008;13(5):1–5. doi: http://dx.doi.org/10.1521/capn.2008.13.5.1

109. Goel R, Hong JS, Findling RL, et al. An update on pharmacotherapy of Autism Spectrum Disorder in children and adolescents. *International Review of Psychiatry* (Abingdon, England) 2018;30(1):78–95. doi: 10.1080/09540261.2018.1458706

110. Gringras P, Nir T, Breddy J, et al. Efficacy and safety of pediatric prolonged-release melatonin for insomnia in children with Autism Spectrum Disorder. *Journal of the American Academy of Child and Adolescent Psychiatry* 2017;56(11):948–57. doi: 10.1016/j.jaac.2017.09.414

111. Politte LC, Howe Y, Nowinski L, et al. Evidence-based treatments for Autism Spectrum Disorder. *Current Treatment Options in Psychiatry* 2015;2(1):38–56. doi: doi:10.1007/s40501-015-0031-z

112. Rydzewska E. Unexpected changes of itinerary – adaptive functioning difficulties in daily transitions for adults with autism spectrum disorder. *European Journal of Special Needs Education* 2016;31(3):330–43. doi:10.1080/08856257.2016. 1187889

113. Smith J, Donlan J, Smith B. *Helping Children with Autism Spectrum Conditions through Everyday Transitions: Small Changes – Big Challenges.* London: Jessica Kingsley; 2012.

114. Uljarević M, Richdale AL, Alexs DW, et al. Interrelationship between insistence on sameness, effortful control and anxiety in adolescents and young adults with autism spectrum disorder (ASD). *Molecular Autism* 2017;8(36) doi: 10.1186/s13229-017-0158-4

115. Sevin JA, Rieske RD, Matson JL. A review of behavioral strategies and support considerations for assisting persons with difficulties transitioning from activity to activity. *Review Journal of Autism and Developmental Disorders* 2015;2:329–42. doi: https://doi.org/10.1007/s40489-015-0056-7

116. Rajendran G, Mitchell P. Cognitive theories of autism. *Developmental Review* 2007;27:224–60. doi: 10.1016/j.dr.2007.02.001

117. Ionescu T. Exploring the nature of cognitive flexibility. *New Ideas in Psychology* 2012;30:190–200. doi: doi:10.1016/j.newideapsych.2011.11.001

118. Brooks A, Schroeder J, Risen JL, et al. Don't stop believing: rituals improve performance by decreasing anxiety. *Organizational Behavior and Human Decision Processes* 2016;137:71–85.

119. De Caluwé EV J, Decuyper M, Bogaerts S, Rettew D, De Clercq B. The relation between normative rituals/routines and obsessive-compulsive symptoms at a young age: A systematic review. *Developmental Review* 2020;56 doi: https://doi.org/10.1016/j.dr.2020.100913

120. Carleton RN. The intolerance of uncertainty construct in the context of anxiety disorders: theoretical and practical perspectives. *Expert Review of Neurotherapeutics* 2012;12(8) doi: 10.1586/ern.12.82

121. Rodgers J, Hodgson A, Shields K, et al. Towards a treatment for intolerance of uncertainty in young people with Autism Spectrum Disorder: development of the Coping with Uncertainty in Everyday Situations (CUES©) programme. *Journal of Autism and Developmental Disorders* 2017;47(12):3959–66. doi: 10.1007/s10803-016-2924-0

122. Rodgers J, Goodwin J, Parr JR, et al. Coping with Uncertainty in Everyday Situations (CUES©) to address intolerance of uncertainty in autistic children: study protocol for an intervention feasibility trial. *Trials* 2019;20(1):385. doi: 10.1186/s13063-019-3479-0

123. Vasa RA, Kreiser NL, Keefer A, et al. Relationships between autism spectrum disorder and intolerance of uncertainty. *Autism Research: Official Journal of the International Society for Autism Research* 2018;11(4):636–44. doi: 10.1002/aur.1916

124. Cumming T, Strnadová I, Danker J. Transitions of students with autism and intellectual disabilities in inclusive settings: the nexus between recommended and actual practice. *Australasian Journal of Special and Inclusive Education* 2021;44(1):28–45. doi:10.1017/jsi.2020.1

125. Lequia J, Wilkerson KL, Kim S, et al. Improving transition behaviors in students with Autism Spectrum Disorders: a comprehensive evaluation of interventions in educational settings. *Journal of Positive Behavior Interventions* 2014;17(3):146–58. doi: 10.1177_1098300714548799

126. Register D, Humpal M. Using musical transitions in early childhood classrooms: three case examples. *Music Therapy Perspectives* 2007;25(1):25–31. doi: 10.1093/mtp/25.1.25

127. Hume KW V, Sam A, Steinbrenner J, Perkins Y, Dees B, Tomaszewski B, Rentschler L, Szendrey S, McIntyre N, White M, Nowell S, Odom S. *Supporting Individuals with Autism through Uncertain Times*. Chapel Hill, NC: School of Education and Frank Porter Graham Child Development Institute, University of North Carolina at Chapel Hill; 2020.

128. Barton E, Harn B. *Educating Young Children with Autism Spectrum Disorders*. Thousand Oaks, California: Corwin, 2012.

129. Wright B, Williams C. *Intervention and Support for Parents and Carers of Children and Young People on the Autism Spectrum: A Resource for Trainers* (Jkp Resource Materials). London: Jessica Kingsley, 2007.

130. Parish SL, Thomas KC, Williams CS, et al. Autism and families' financial burden: the association with health insurance coverage. *American Journal on Intellectual and Developmental Disabilities* 2015;120(2):166–75. doi: 10.1352/1944-7558-120.2.166

131. Paula CS, Cukier S, Cunha GR, et al. Challenges, priorities, barriers to care, and stigma in families of people with autism: Similarities and differences among six Latin American countries. *Autism: the International Journal of Research and Practice* 2020;24(8):2228-42. doi: 10.1177/1362361320940073

132. Sharpe DL, Baker DL. Financial issues associated with having a child with autism. *Journal of Family and Economic Issues* 2007;28(2):247–64. doi: doi:10.1007/s10834-007-9059-6

133. Roddy A, O'Neill C. The economic costs and its predictors for childhood autism spectrum disorders in Ireland: How is the burden distributed? *Autism: the International Journal of Research and Practice* 2019;23(5):1106–18. doi:10.1177/1362361318801586

134. Raz R, Lerner-Geva L, Leon O, et al. A survey of out-of-pocket expenditures for children with autism spectrum disorder in Israel. *Journal of Autism and Developmental Disorders* 2013;43(10):2295-302. doi: 10.1007/s10803-013-1782-2

135. Chan KKS, Leung DCK. The impact of child autistic symptoms on parental marital relationship: parenting and coparenting processes as mediating mechanisms. *Autism Research: Official Journal of the International Society for Autism Research* 2020;13(9):1516-26. doi: 10.1002/aur.2297

136. Hartley SL, Papp LM, Bolt D. Spillover of marital interactions and parenting stress in families of children with Autism Spectrum Disorder. *Journal of Clinical Child and Adolescent Psychology: the Official Journal for the Society of Clinical Child and Adolescent Psychology, American Psychological Association, Division 53* 2018;53(47(sup1)):S88–S99. doi: 10.1080/15374416.2016.1152552

137. Grebe SC, Mire SS, Kim H, et al. Comparing fathers' and mothers' perspectives about their child's Autism Spectrum Disorder. *Journal of Autism and Developmental Disorders* 2021 doi: 10.1007/s10803-021-05077-7

138. Foody C, James JE, Leader G. Parenting stress, salivary biomarkers, and ambulatory blood pressure: a comparison between mothers and fathers of children

with autism spectrum disorders. *Journal of Autism and Developmental Disorders* 2015;45(4):1084–95. doi: 10.1007/s10803-014-2263-y

139. Green L. The well-being of siblings of individuals with autism. *International Scholarly Research Notices* 2013;417194 doi: 10.1155/2013/417194

140. Ferraioli SJ, Harris SL. The impact of autism on siblings. *Social Work in Mental Health* 2009;8(1):41-53. doi: Social Work in Mental Health, Vol. 8, No. 1, January–February 2010: pp. 41–53

141. Kovshoff H, Cebula K, Tsai HJ, et al. Siblings of children with autism: the Siblings Embedded Systems Framework. *Current Developmental Disorders Reports* 2017;4(2):37-45. doi: 10.1007/s40474-017-0110-5

142. Hartley SL, Schultz HM. Support needs of fathers and mothers of children and adolescents with autism spectrum disorder. *Journal of Autism and Developmental Disorders* 2015;45(6):1636-48. doi: 10.1007/s10803-014-2318-0

143. Karp EA, Kuo AA. Maternal mental health after a child's diagnosis of autism spectrum disorder. *Journal of the American Medical Association* 2015;313(1):81–2. doi: 10.1001/jama.2014.11187

144. Hsiao YJ. Pathways to mental health-related quality of life for parents of children with autism spectrum disorder: roles of parental stress, children's performance, medical support, and neighbor support. *Research Autism Spectrum Disorders* 2016;23:122–30.

145. Kuhlthau KP N., Delahaye J, Hurson J, Pyne J, Kovacs E, Tilford M. Quality of life for parents of children with autism spectrum disorders. *Research in Autism Spectrum Disorders* 2014;8(10) doi: doi.org/10.1016/j.rasd.2014.07.002

146. Solomon AH, Chung B. Understanding autism: how family therapists can support parents of children with Autism Spectrum Disorders. *Family Process* 2012;51(2):250–64. doi: 10.1111/j.1545-5300.2012.01399.x

147. Jellett R, Wood CE, Giallo R, et al. Family functioning and behaviour problems in children with Autism Spectrum Disorders: The mediating role of parent mental health. *Clinical Psychologist* 2015;19(1):39-48. doi: 10.1111/cp.12047

148. Cai RY, Uljarević M, Leekam SR. Predicting mental health and psychological wellbeing in mothers of children with Autism Spectrum Disorder: roles of intolerance of uncertainty and coping. *Autism Research: Official Journal of the International Society for Autism Research* 2020;13(10):1797–801. doi: 10.1002/aur.2341

149. Roughan LA, Parker JR, Mercer L. Improving interventions for parents of children and young people with autism spectrum disorder (ASD) in CAMHS. *British Medical Journal Open Qualitative* 2019;8(2):e000261. doi: 10.1136/bmjoq-2017-000261

150. Stošić J, Skrinjar JF, Preece D. Families of children on the autism spectrum: experience of daily life and impact of parent education. *Support for Learning* 2020;35:205–21. doi: https://doi.org/10.1111/1467-9604.12300

151. Farmer J, Reupert A. Understanding autism and understanding my child with autism: an evaluation of a group parent education program in rural Australia. *Australian Journal of Rural Health* 2013;21(1):20-7. doi: 10.1111/ajr.12004

152. MacDonald A. *Solution-Focused Therapy: Theory, Research and Practice*. London: Sage Publications Ltd; 2nd ed, 2011.

153. Bowen M. Introduction to the eight concepts. The Bowen Centre for the Study of the Family. 2021 [internet]. Available from: https://www.thebowencenter.org/introduction-eight-concepts

154. Rogers CR. *Client-centered Therapy*. Houghton Mifflin; 1951.

155. Wickman SAC, C. An analysis of how Carl Rogers enacted client-centred conversation with Gloria. *Journal of Counseling & Development* 2003;81:178–84. doi: https://doi.org/10.1002/j.1556-6678.2003.tb00239.x

156. Bradford K. Supporting families dealing with autism and Asperger's disorders. *Journal of Family Psychotherapy* 2010;21(2):149–56. doi: Journal of Family Psychotherapy, Vol. 21, No. 2, April–June 2010: pp 149–156.

157. Boshoff K, Gibbs D, Phillips RL, et al. Parents' voices: 'Our process of advocating for our child with autism.' A meta-synthesis of parents' perspectives. *Child: Care, Health and Development* 2018;44(1):147–60. doi: 10.1111/cch.12504

158. Brookman-Frazee L, Koegel RL. Using parent/clinician partnerships in parent education programs for children with autism. *Journal of Positive Behaviour Interventions* 2004;6(4):195–213. doi: 10.1177_10983007040060040201

159. Vlcek S, Somerton M, Rayner C. Collaborative teams: teachers, parents, and allied health professionals supporting students with Autism Spectrum Disorder in mainstream Australian schools. *Australasian Journal of Special and Inclusive Education* 2020;44(2):102–15. doi: doi:10.1017/jsi.2020.11

160. Goldman SE, Burke MM. The perceptions of school involvement of parents of students with Autism Spectrum Disorders: a systematic literature review. *Review Journal of Autism and Developmental Disorders* 2019;6(2):109–27. doi:10.1007/s40489-019-00157-y

161. Whitaker P. Supporting families of preschool children with autism: what parents want and what helps. *Autism: the International Journal of Research and Practice* 2002;6(4):411–26. doi: 10.1177/1362361302006004007

162. Elder JH, D'Alessandro T. Supporting families of children with autism spectrum disorders: questions parents ask and what nurses need to know. *Peadiatric Nursing* 2009;35(4):240–5,53.

163. Collin K, Van der Heijden B, Lewis P. Continuing professional development. *International Journal of Training and Development* 2012;16(3):155–63. doi: 10.1111/j.1468-2419.2012.00410.x

164. Price S, Reichert C. The importance of continuing professional development to career satisfaction and patient care: meeting the needs of novice to mid- to late-career nurses throughout their career span. *Administrative Sciences* 2017;7(2):17. doi: 10.3390/admsci7020017

165. Mintz J, Seleznyov S, Peacey N, et al. Evidence informed practice for autism, special educational needs and disability in schools: expanding the scope of the research learning community model of professional development. *Support for Learning* 2021;36(2):159–82. doi: http://dx.doi.org/10.1111/1467-9604.12349